Maybe Not Such a Good Girl

Reflections on Rupture and Return

by Susan Reimer-Torn

Blue Thread Communications

For information, write to: JEWISH CURRENTS, PO Box 111, Accord, NY 12404.

ISBN 978-0-9890000-6-2

Maybe Not Such a Good Girl

Reflections on Rupture and Return

TAIKU

A Prelude

Miss Liberty

Still, I wonder how I have gotten from there to here.

My husband wonders why I am so withdrawn. Like a prodding parent, he wishes I would show off my early education. It is true that I can read Aramaic and my Hebrew is altogether literate, but on this day I choose to be silent. Invisibility, were it possible in this unsparing light, would suit my mood even better.

Those of us gathered here are accustomed to meeting in shoddier surroundings, subterranean community rooms that double as homeless shelters at night. Here on the 38th floor of a midtown skyscraper, the unfiltered light, the steel, the glass, and our defiantly lofty perch set a more challenging tone.

How has it come to this? What is happening to me, the zealot's runaway daughter, and E.T., my Jewishly unaffiliated, French-educated husband? Why have we come to a midweek lunchtime Talmud class, hosted in the glass-walled conference room of one of New York City's most muscular law firms?

There is, of course, the appeal of the teacher, Rabbi Roly, the sweet and soulful, soccer-mad Argentinean import, the liberal Upper West Side's version of a *wunder rebbe,* and the irresistible course title he has chosen: "Perversion and Holiness, Stories of the Talmudic Rabbis."

The last time I beheld a Talmudic text was some forty years ago, when I was 17 and cramming for my final high school exam — not having followed a word the Talmud teacher said for weeks, but counting on my best friend Lilah to decode the crowded, squiggly black letters into streams of logic in a couple of pre-exam all-nighters. She did so faithfully, as I knew she would, both of us sprawled on the floor of my bedroom amid graham cracker and pretzel crumbs. Kneeling over the weighty tome, Lilah drew for me a coherent pathway through the cryptic, tortuously circuitous text, and did not mind when I managed to match her own fine score in the next morning's exam.

We parted after senior year, she going off to Israel, me following a more conventional path to college and then later to France. A decade ago, I was still living in France, and Lilah was dying of brain cancer in Florida. We were on the phone, Ft. Lauderdale to Paris, discussing details of her upcoming burial.

Ever practical, about to enter hospice care, Lilah is in need of help with a logistical problem. A single mom of three daughters, a survivor of breast cancer, she had years before purchased her burial plot in New Jersey, taking advantage of "a good deal." She quietly explains that since she now lives in Florida, after her burial up north the girls will have no place to sit the first few days of *shiva*. Of course, I tell her they can use my place in Manhattan. She warns me: Her middle daughter, 26, pregnant and the mother of three, is married to a fiercely pious *ba'al teshuva,* a humorless, take-no-prisoners, born-again Jew. He will no doubt commandeer my place and the proceedings; her daughters and I will have nothing to say. Lilah is speaking to me in a calm, deliberate voice, the way she might have in the past when explaining a subtle point of law (she became an attorney later in life) or when asking me to arrange a hotel stay in Paris or a heart-healthy meal for a visiting relative.

Her calm urges me not to resist the present moment, to settle into it with what meditation teachers call mindfulness or equanimity. You get to practice mindfulness when something overwhelming comes up and you pause to deepen the breath, to let the inhalation expand your belly and, along with the in-breath, to let your sorrow or your fear or your anger or your anguish reach its apex and then, because you have allowed it, because you have made space, because eventually you do exhale, you get to watch the pain of even the deepest cut slowly fade in intensity. Not everyone wants to try this; sometimes, though, it's the only resort. I reply to Lilah in Hebrew, and my words are halting, only partly due to the French that has more recently been overlaid on my second-language track.

"Of course, *b'seder,* however you want it to be."

She is amazingly lucid for someone whose brain has been invaded by unshrinkable tumors. She reminds me that I will have to find high necklines, low hemlines, and long sleeves. We laugh about the imperative to hide "our irresistible elbows and knees," even more so "our incendiary armpits." Her son-in-law, I must understand, will erect a makeshift *mechitza* in my living room to separate the men and women. She warns me there may well be times when the zealot deems it unacceptable for women to appear at all. I see myself banished to the hinterlands of my own apartment by a dark-bearded, 28-year-old kid glowering at me from under his brimmed black hat. And, though I don't ask, I am certain there will be no option for any of us lowly *nekevot*, females, to recite the *kaddish.* The son-in-law, a newcomer to Orthodoxy, will be the self-appointed proxy to hastily mumble the prayer that shepherds Lilah's soul to the higher spheres, while the three daughters she singlehandedly raised will be obediently silent.

I assure her all will go as she wishes. Then I am silent in anticipation of all that is to come.

"Suzi?

"I'm here."

"Just take it lightly." And after a pause, "Have a good laugh on me and the irony of life."

It comes as no surprise that Lilah and I confer on end-of-life matters: We always shared our defining moments going back to girlhood. At first, the urge to defy the Orthodoxy in which we were raised felt like a subterranean rumble, an undertow to which we could only allude in tentative whispers. As soon as we dared a little taboo-busting (who can forget the first electric light defiantly switched on during the Sabbath day), the tug turned into a riptide that carried us further from the safety of familiar shores, faster and more irreversibly than we ever intended.

We were 17 when Lilah and I met that Sunday on Upper Broadway for a premeditated foray into the forbidden. It was a blustery autumn day, the clocks had been turned back, and the withered leaves were being whipped up into a circle dance by the chilly winds off the Hudson. We hooked eyes over a streaky Formica table in the recesses of a Four Brothers coffee shop.

"You haven't changed your mind?"

Lilah shook her kinky, dark curls.

"You're doing it because you want to, right, not because of me?"

Lilah nodded, her blue eyes dilating behind her thick-rimmed glasses.

I steeled myself on her non-contrite expression, hoping mine was equally unflinching. Lilah paused to douse her burger with ketchup, as if she were already well established in the routine. Then, on unspoken cue, we raised the non-kosher hamburgers toward virgin lips. As she dropped her jaw and my lips parted, in unison, we introduced our first morsel of non-kosher food to mouths heretofore unsullied by forbidden fare.

We knew that breaking away meant closing our eyes and taking the greasy plunge, stopping our hearts from exploding and sticking out our thumbs. Next it was a Sabbath afternoon in early spring, and this time we were daring to hitchhike all the way into Manhattan, while our families assumed we were just out for a walk in the quiet Queens neighborhood where everyone from our world was sleepwalking in a full-bellied Sabbath haze. We speed-walked several blocks out of the parameters of the many *shabbos* strollers towards a main thoroughfare. I stepped out into the street and, just to make Lilah laugh, raised my skirt to show off my ankles the way we'd seen naughty girls do in old films.

A low-slung Chevy skidded to a stop. The driver was wearing a battered leather jacket strewn with cigarette ashes.

"Where ya headed, girls?"

"We don't really know," I said.

"We just wanna go that way," Lilah offered, pointing to the skyline across the river.

"Goin' nowhere fast, huh?" The guy smiled in an understanding way.

He said he was crossing the bridge into Manhattan, and that sounded to us like just the right thing. We moved fast to not lose our nerve, scrambled into the back seat, and squeezed each other's hands as the car levitated over the East River. We were flying over a bridge, crossing the Great Divide, soaring across the sparkling water. In the back seat, stuffing was popping out of a rip in the upholstery, and I imagined someone slashing it with a knife, maybe in the heat of a scuffle. Out there on the other bank of the river, clearly visible from the bridge, the skyscrapers of downtown Manhattan gleamed like gates of a forbidden city.

As soon as we touched down in Manhattan, we scurried to the subway to make our way back home from the Other Side. We arrived just in time for the *havdala* service separating the holy Sabbath from the other days of the week. If they knew what we had just done, they would be separating us out from all that is sacred. Lilah brandished the braided candle high, not flinching even when the wax drippings singed her tightly clenched fingers. She reminded me of Miss Liberty, ample, grounded, reassuring yet defiant, holding her torch high in the midst of all that shimmering water.

From my perch on the 38th floor, with a photocopied page of Talmud and its English translation spread before me this lunch hour, I can again glimpse Miss Liberty way out there in the harbor. I'm quiet because I'm remembering studying for the Talmud final and the crumbly hamburger and the first time we dared ride in a car on the Sabbath. I remember, too, how when Lilah got to Israel after high school graduation, she gave birth to — and was immediately forced to give up — the girl baby she only discovered she was carrying once she was far from home. Birth and obligatory adoption: After that, she hastily married a shiftless Romanian handyman with whom she shared no spoken language. He promised to help her get her baby back, but he never did. Within three years, she mothered three more daughters, and before long she was raising them on her own.

By the time Lilah was nearly 50, long divorced, battling her second bout of cancer, two of her three daughters had returned to Orthodoxy. The eldest, Shira, who did most of the hands-on caregiving when Lilah got sick, was not (yet) so inclined. Shira, her mom, and I had shared many sweet moments. Their home in Southern Florida had been my haven from many a sunless European winter over the years. Shira and I would bike-ride and roller-blade along the funky Hollywood boardwalk, find a secluded place to smoke a joint and listen to the Grateful Dead, then swim out in long strokes beyond the waves, while Lilah, tickled by our intergenerational friendship, and waiting with a book and ample snacks, would mommy my own two little boys under an oversized umbrella near the shore.

In December of that millennium year, I was back in New York, visiting from France, when Shira called from Florida to tell me Lilah had decided to stop taking her meds. Lilah knew the situation was beyond the help of medical science and saw no reason to burden her final days with a regimen of pharmaceuticals. I told a panicked Shira to respect her mother's decision; Lilah had always carved her own path. We would be leaving her this dignity of choice, even if it shortened what was left of her life.

For the first time since I was a teenager in summer camp, I began attending Friday-night services whenever I found myself visiting from France on the Upper West Side (where I had always held on to my rent-stabilized apartment from my student days). I would stand in the back row of the balcony of a synagogue called BJ, short for B'nai Jeshurun. BJ's Friday-night sessions were so well attended that overflow crowds had to be accommodated in two services held in a large Methodist-Episcopalian church across the avenue from my apartment.

At BJ, I would hear a song whose words I understood but whose meaning eluded me. A great Hasidic leader, Rabbi Nachman of Bratslov, wrote it, and I recall that Jews were known to sing it on their way to the gas chambers. The lyric says: *This entire world is a very narrow bridge, and the main thing is not to fear anything at all.* I would think of myself trying to find a bridge back to my native New York City after all the years away in France. I would think of Lilah on that narrowest of bridges from this world to the next. I would wonder what it implied that the passageway was, according to this mystical mind, so exceptionally narrow.

I returned once again to New York City from Paris in time for Lilah's New Jersey burial. I put on a long, though not shapeless, skirt and covered my head with a gold-and-turquoise Lanvin-print scarf that Lilah had once offered me as a gift. For three days, I gave my home over to the tribe of loveless black-hats and, as promised, made not a peep of protest. Although the men's eyes never met mine, their surly coldness declared their resentment — or was it confusion? — over the unfathomable decision of God, in whose volunteer army they served 24/7, to inflict them with ungovernable females. They yanked and clunked the antique couch that sat against the wall into a makeshift *mechitza*, diagonally cutting the living room in half. Although my kitchen was vegetarian, every morsel of food was wrapped in layers of aluminum while some woman kept my stove burners lit for hours to burn away any impurity.

One night, Liz, the cat I was keeping for a friend, wandered out and took up her perch on the displaced sofa. Liz was old and ornery, conditioned to fighting off foes, real or imagined. Weeks before the *shiva*, she had claimed that corner of the sofa as her rightful place. Not one of the men could stand up to her snarling refusal to be displaced. That night, wearing quilted mitts, I had to scoop her up before one of the men kicked her in her sagging belly.

Another night, the intercom gave out and a bearded man stationed himself like a brooding sentry in the lobby; my discomfited neighbors shared the elevator with legions of black-vested men. There was never a word of gratitude from the black-hats, though Lilah's three girls constantly expressed their thanks.

"Suzi," I kept telling myself, "do like she said, just take it lightly; enjoy the irony, have a good laugh on life."

All through that first lunchtime Talmud class, I'm thinking about the good laugh, the last laugh, the good life, Miss Liberty, and the pursuit of happiness. I'm thinking about that ornery Liz and the narrow bridge, wondering if there might ever be one spanning opposing worldviews — and I remember my friend Lilah and me holding hands in the back seat, soaring high over the waters.

I for Impurity

I'm not sure if the Talmudic material we are studying with Rabbi Roly is what I would call perverse, but it certainly is highly unusual. In the 7th chapter of the Bava Metzia tractate, we are introduced to a revered rabbinic teacher who has an innocent man arrested and then cuts off his own flesh to see if it will rot in the sun. He declares the non-rot to be proof of his vindication in the nasty affair. Then there's a rabbi who preens like a peacock in front of women emerging from the *mikve*, the ritual bath. The women are now fit to resume relations with their husband, and the preener insists he is there to encourage amorous feelings within couples. What's more, he is convinced that the sight of his own beauty will make such an imprint on the passing women that it will foster the birth of beautiful babies.

Who says that Judaism is not susceptible to narcissism or tinged with magical thinking, that it is not varied and colorful in its folklore? Following that, some rabbis indulge in a bragging contest about the size of their sex organs.

They must have been exceptionally bored that day.

I remember how, back in high school, our small, rotund Talmud teacher would raise his voice and even start a strange swaying left to right to keep up our interest in this musty labyrinth of endless hermetic arguments. We were ushered into a world of nuanced

9

debates over such matters as requisite damages owed by one man when another man's straying cow falls into his uncovered pit. It was impossible to perceive even a glimmer of relevant connection between the obsessions of sages long dead and the mind-bending psychedelia erupting all around us in the late '60s. Throughout the ninety-minute high school class, my mind, refusing to commit brain cells to the laborious ins and outs of Talmudic logic, would instead succumb to a blank monotonous buzz. Now, some forty years later, having raised my children in a foreign land, having put as much distance as I could between my past and myself, I am here with other perfectly functional, open-minded adults, returning in the middle of a working day in midtown to a consideration of these ancient texts.

Next comes the passage in which the reputation of Rabbi Eleazar, son of Rabbi Simeon, is impugned by the carelessness with which he performs one of his many Jewish legal duties. This particular halachic duty has to do with the authorization of sexual intercourse between married couples after the obligatory period of abstinence during and following a woman's menstrual flow. According to Orthodox Jewish law, marital relations are strictly forbidden during menstruation and for seven days afterwards. At the conclusion of the seven days, suspicious specimens of vaginal discharge must be presented for the okay of the community rabbi. In this case, Rabbi Eleazar is suspected of having too hastily approved specimens of questionable purity. He counters with proof of his rigor: In each and every case, sixty in all, the couple resumed relations and nine months later were the proud parents of a new baby boy. (And all sixty, Eleazar adds, were named after him!)

There is some murmured confusion among Roly's lunchtime students. As is so often the case when it comes to decoding Talmudic associations, connections are not always clear — but in this case they are crystal clear to me. I speak up loudly, and for the first time: Had the post-menstrual discharge been ritually unclean, the dire result of Eleazar's carelessness would have been the birth of a baby girl rather than the coveted boy. Roly (himself the father of two daughters and no sons) ruefully confirms the accuracy of my observation. It is true, if surely lamentable, that females, according to Talmudic tradition, are the living result of haste and transgression. We arise from impurity; our essence is the issue of a bloodstain.

This is not the first time I have heard this precious droplet of rabbinical wisdom, but it has been many years since it's arisen in my awareness. Much earlier on, it must have burrowed its way into my deeper recesses and left its indelible association of female body with sin.

I remember how I violated the Sabbath, intentionally and for the very first time. It happened behind closed doors in the cramped bathroom the whole family shared, the one with the sunflower wallpaper my mom and I had chosen. I am waiting for the last drops of urine to drop into the bowl when I realize we've run out of the toilet paper pre-torn for the Sabbath day. (Tearing of paper is one of the many acts of labor forbidden on the Sabbath.) I do have an alternative: I can get up and reach for the tissue dispenser on the opposite wall. But just next to me, easily within reach, is a roll of uncut toilet paper. The idea intrudes like a snake poking its head out of a hole. Temptation grips me and I rip the paper off the roll. Slowly, deliberately, I rub the paper against my moist vagina. As I flush the evidence away, the waters rush with a dizzying thrill.

Rage

I am not sure how the others sitting around the big conference table, with paper plates piled with fruit salad and bloated tea bags, relate to these bizarre Talmudic tales, but I'm beginning to appreciate the unflinching honesty of the compilers. There's one in which the preening rabbi and his spiritual son, a repentant thief, suddenly begin insulting each other over a minor legalistic dispute. Repressed anger and long-buried resentment erupt into a quarrel that results in the illness (both mental and physical) of both protagonists and their untimely deaths. The men expire from heartache, from an overdose of unconscious passions and a sad inability to forgive.

I can't gauge how many of the assembled would know of such dangerously repressed emotions triggering wild explosions of wrath. Having grown up with my father, having withstood his uncontrollable rages and dreading his radical mood swings, I know of it all too well.

Mine was not the only Orthodox father who struggled with emotional disequilibrium and unmanageable anger. He was not the only pious devotee who periodically, at terrifyingly unpredictable intervals, flipped out. Many of those most revered for their leadership in working-class Orthodox communities had a fiercely furious dark side. They clung to their religious practice like Odysseus tied to the mast, binding themselves with leather *tfillin* straps against spasmodic bursts of aggression.

There was, for example, my friend Hesh's father, the revered, white-robed, guest rabbi from Yeshiva University who deigned to lead our modest but fervent community in the High Holiday services each year. I remember him rushing by in august rabbinical haste, tall and flushed, securing the cord around his white, flowing robes. Later on, during my teen years, tragic news passed through our community about this revered High Holiday guest rabbi: He had lost his first-born son, Hesh's older brother, on the operating table, where the surgeons had hoped to repair the boy's congenital heart ailment. Then, in a nightmarish incident, his younger son Hesh had been jumped by some Puerto Rican hoodlums and beaten so badly that he was laid up for days.

It would not have occurred to Hesh and me to speak to one another in those early days, or even to look one another in the eye over the great gender divide. Fast-forward a decade or two, and we found ourselves romantically involved as members of an ad hoc mid-

'70s subculture of lost souls who had left their Orthodox upbringings behind — all of us unmoored, floating like lone doves, Chagall-like through a kaleidoscopic wonderland of a world, wondering where, after the deluge, we might land.

Hesh and I . . . we had our ways. We scoured the underground of New York in the '70s, catching one another up on the inner linings of our lives. He told me of his father's inconsolable sorrow, turned to brutal rage, over the loss of "the wrong son." It was the rabbi, not the Puerto Ricans, who had beaten Hesh to a pulp, this because Hesh had managed to confuse God Himself in His cruel choice of brothers, this because the devilish boy had dared to be spared.

Hesh knew Lilah from the old days of our original disaffection, and he met her again during his winter sojourns in Florida where he went to nurse a weak heart of his own. Hesh made an appearance at my home during the *shiva* for Lilah (even though at that time Hesh, who never married, was miffed at me for some undisclosed slight). My son Raphael was spending his freshman college year in New York City, enjoying this new multiculturalism after his more homogeneous upbringing in France. He could not fathom what had possessed me to allow for the three-day "Taliban take-over."

"Mom," my son protested with incredulity, "they don't even respect you."

I was in no position to explain. Hesh was the one with whom I communicated without either one of us uttering a word. He and I both knew there were times when it was best to be silent.

The Other

Another of our Talmud classes opens with a story I once heard long ago. In the middle of a steamy night, sitting halfway up in our rumpled bed, Hesh told me the story of the Acher, an esteemed religious leader who abruptly turns apostate. Now, in the sterility of a corporate conference room so many years later, the long-forgotten tale is retold.

Ever since Elisha ben Abuyah, a once-revered rabbi, lost his faith, he came to be known as "the Acher" or the Other. One Saturday afternoon, the Acher flamboyantly rides through town in defiance of the Sabbath laws. So hungry is his student Rabbi Meier for words of Torah from the mouth of his former teacher, the breathless disciple runs alongside the horse, lost in urgent discussion and oblivious to time and space. Of the two, it is the renegade Acher who has not neglected to carefully measure the distance covered by the strides of his horse in awareness of the permitted Sabbath boundary. When he knows they are about to exceed it, the Acher excitedly cautions Rabbi Meier to turn back. As for the Acher, still riding high, he transgresses the boundary. He offers an explanation: A *bat kol,* a voice from the hidden sphere beyond the veil, has called out to all erring children to return — all errants, the voice specified, except the Acher.

Hesh and I, two self-exiles from the parameters of Orthodox Jewry, shared a fascination for the figure of the Acher. Here is a revered and righteous leader whose faith is eradicated. He is unabashed in his display of profligacy. Yet his depth of wisdom is so unique that a student destined to be a great man still wants to study with him, even if he has to trot breathlessly alongside horse and rider on the Sabbath day. When they reach the Sabbath limits, the Acher, a man of lapsed faith, passionately urges that Meier not be brought to sin unwittingly and on his account. But if the Acher truly does not believe in the authority of rabbinic law, why would he care about Meier's transgression? What stops him from urging his student to throw off the yoke and join him on the other side?

The paradoxical nature of belief/non-belief is deepened by the Acher's relationship with the *bat kol* or the heavenly voice from behind the veil. How can the outlook of a great sage who has renounced the abiding authority of God still be influenced by a voice presumed to emanate from God's abode? Why does such a message hold him in its sway? The Acher adheres to the voice's message — one that seals his irreversible fate as an apostate — with the same certainty with which he has rejected the tenets of the Jewish faith. I remember how Hesh and I loved to get entangled in these sorts of impossible contradictions between making love in the wee hours.

In the midday, law-office Talmud class, I learn something about the Acher I had not known before: that Rabbi Meier's continuing devotion to his heretical master is questioned by some and justified by others. Meier's defenders compare the Acher to a pomegranate; it is suggested that perhaps Acher's essence did not change, only his exterior. From that perspective, the radically devoted Rabbi Meier ate only of the Acher's internal seeds while knowing enough to throw away the peel.

Does the distinction between the inner and the outer person suggest that certain emotional quirks, inadvertent traumas, personality-linked traits, or otherwise-transitory determinants of our nature allow certain people to steadily maintain faith while making it impossible for others? Can it be that the souls of those who in their temporal existence stray from observance may remain untainted in their essence? Lilah, Hesh, and I spent many hours exploring what it was that made us different from those in our community who never strayed.

Our awakening intellects constructed well-reasoned arguments against the basic tenets of Orthodox faith. Our youthful zest for living burst the narrow confines of the permitted. The late '60s deconstructed all previous cultural assumptions, and a deadening, doubt-riddled faith was no match for a world in the throes of turning on, dropping out, and loving freely. There were those who lived out the upheavals with their ingrained commitment to Judaism unchanged. (There were, after all, those who survived the death camps with their ingrained commitment unchanged.) There were others who were involved early on, in the late '60s and early '70s, with pioneering attempts to revive the tradition. But we wanted no part of it. What accounted for rebel-hearts like ours, what made it impossible for us to draw near, to heed the commandment to love God and obey His law?

I spent the first phase of my adulthood, twenty-two years of it, living in France. During those decades, I deliberately put distance between the American Jewish scene and myself. Yet since my return to my native New York in 2001, I have found myself increasingly drawn to Jewish communal life, with all its spiritual, intellectual, and social concerns. Mine is a story of rupture and return, an evolving, possibly even revolving, tale. I live this story every day with a radical sense of amazement.

Rabbi Roly is saying that sometimes there is in the Talmud a contro-versy among colleagues that cannot be resolved. I hear myself saying *"TAIKU"* out loud, along with him. During the all-night study sessions with Lilah, somewhere at around 2:00 in the morning, after a piti-lessly long trek through the maze of each player's particular take on legal logic, the spirited yet unsparing intellectual jousting would sometimes wind down into a carefully wrought consensus. Other times, no matter from how many angles the matter was considered, it was not possible to come to an agreement; all sides had argued the merits of their irreconcilable positions to the point of stalemate. In these instances, the sages would invoke a single word to relieve the over-stimulated cortex: *TAIKU.*

Roly is explaining that *TAIKU* is an acronym for the coming of Elijah, he who will someday answer all questions and resolve all disputes. In fact, there is a traditional myth that each of us will be granted the privilege of asking Elijah one question, just one. I will ask Elijah to help me find meaning in my still-unfolding life journey. Until his coming, all we can do is clumsily conduct our own investigations into the mysteries of individual journeys, purpose, and fate.

Both Lilah and Hesh died in their mid-50s. Neither one of my fellow escapees lived long enough for me to share with them my return to lunchtime Talmud classes, but neither would have been surprised. Like the Acher, not one of us could consider resuming an Orthodox way of life. Still, we would have enjoyed a late-night discussion about the pomegranate and the Jewish Question. We might have ended the discussion with the invocation of *TAIKU*. We profligates would return to the big questions again and again, never subscribing to binding replies. We knew that the call of an ultimate concern is not so easily silenced. There is a *bat kol* from behind the veil, an audible voice, beckoning and broken, haunting and harsh, that always remains.

You Who Love My Soul

Part One

Sehnsucht

I can't shed my misgivings about the ready smiles. Whereas others turn to community as an antidote to isolation, I have a nasty history of rupture with all that beckons here. Already I am in far deeper than I ever intended. In my personal history, Judaism is an arena of conflict and strife, of my parents' unreasonable demands and hideously dashed expectations. It took all of my courage to fight my way out of Orthodoxy and then keep myself intact in spite of my family's heartbreak and censure. I made the firm decision, decades ago, not to get near any of this ever again.

Now in mid-life, after decades of self-exile, under no coercion, with both my parents gone, my two French-born children grown, and in response to no external authority, week after week, to my own amazement, *hineni*, my long-lost brothers and sisters: I am here, taking up an aisle seat at a West Side synagogue called B'nai Jeshurun. This is not a faithful copy of the Orthodox synagogues of my childhood: At BJ, men and women sit together, women go up to the Torah, and one of the three rabbis is a never-been-married mom. Still, the liturgy, the reading, and the melodies are so unchanged as to powerfully evoke the past. What am I seeking here, back at the scene of a primordial rift? How has a tentative exploration of a neighborhood synagogue morphed into a compelling weekly routine?

Were it not for my past, would I be here at all? I cannot say. Were it not for my past, might I be more upfront and personal, with fewer self-imposed constraints? Probably. I come to BJ services dragging my weighty baggage: In the beginning there was total childhood devotion, then reckless adolescent rebellion. Until now, there has been little in my experience of an in-between, little that I could call my own, a grown-up, self-generated religious response free of reactivity to circumstances.

After fierce loyalty and spiteful betrayal, can I possibly come to the center? After all that has come to pass in childhood and adolescence, might I now cobble together such a thing as a happy Jewish adulthood? If so, with what sort of synthesized version of Judaism would I align? Assuming I find my own way, will the rewards be sufficiently life-enhancing to outweigh the risks? What exactly are the risks? Some part of me is drawn to this midlife wager, while another is deeply suspicious. Then there's another part of me — cautious, observant, curious, and baffled — that has agreed to go along for the ride.

On those first Friday nights, I climb way up in the balcony and always carefully choose an aisle seat, in case I need to escape. My pockets are stuffed with tissues, though I don't have a cold. My eyes are closed, and heaviness lifts as soft warmth spreads inside. I draw the words in deeper, then exhale them into every tight spot in my body. Can it be, after decades of exile and determined flight, of never knowing where I might land, that I am now on safe ground? Can I really settle in here? Melodies weave a spiral of new possibilities. I can dip and twist, I can sway, wander, and whirl. Does that mean the door is still open for me, even after all this time away? Where will I locate myself, what will be my reference points once I enter this portal?

Behind closed eyes, I imagine that each song is an unseen partner in a new dance. A keyboard, a cello, and a flute accompany us, while a djembe player keeps the rhythm with the help of a rustling tambourine. Each phrase, taken from the Psalms or the Song of Songs or the traditional liturgy, is familiar from childhood. I don't need to read the words, for I have never forgotten them. They are sustained by a thousand voices gathered in a neighborhood church to usher in the Sabbath Bride. But now the same words dissolve and reform, refracting with a thousand new meanings. *Ve'taher libainu l'uvdecha be'emet:* Purify our hearts to worship You in truth. Purify. Truth. Heart. Our. You. Yours. Worship. Heart. Truth. Yours. Mine. Ours. Something inside wants to unstring and restring these words into endless possibilities, to follow them wherever they may lead.

Precarious, I say to myself, a word that I recently discovered is related to prayer itself, hence to all that is uncertain, all that depends on circumstances, all that is risky and dangerous, beyond our control. I am powerfully drawn to this gathering, to its choreographed ceremony and precarious devotion. Meanwhile, my danger sensors, self-appointed guardians of my emotional preserve, are blinking on alert.

Attraction/repulsion: I have indulged these polarities in the past, leaving behind all that offered a more demure buzz. Am I, in midlife, revisiting a youthful zest for living on the edge? On a Sabbath eve, I greet the old pattern in its coy new guise from my perch in a synagogue balcony.

Back in the Beforetime, there was a Friday-night song that my father and I sang in harmony every week. *"Yedid Nefesh,"* recently translated as "You Who Love My Soul," expresses a mystical longing for union with God. For years, my father and I would interweave our voices in a shared plea for the sweetness of God's soul-healing light.

Before long, the words to the Friday-night song turned sour. *"Yedid Nefesh"* was no longer a plea for closeness to the Divine, but a desperate supplication that I be cured of the evil inclination that had me increasingly in its sway. *Ah na el na,* I beseech you God, *refah na la,* please do heal her. My father's eyes would brim with tears. He was dissolving, and with him the pillar that held up the sky. He was undone by the knowledge that I was drifting away, and he prayed to God to heal me of this perversity in my soul.

One Friday night, I arrive at BJ a few minutes before the start of the service, rather than my usual ten or fifteen minutes after it has begun. When the crowd settles into a hush and the first keyboard notes are sounded, I discover that *"Yedid Nefesh"* is the opening song, harmonized in the same melody I shared with my father. I am hearing this song for the first time in nearly forty years. It reverberates in hollow places inside, while my voice has no resonance. It has turned into pure breath, and I cannot join in with the others.

I only start showing up at BJ on Saturday mornings, in addition to Friday nights, in the eleven months following my mother's death. Safety dictates that at first I only take it upon myself to get there in time for the mourner's *kaddish*, which comes at the very end of the three-hour service. (Here in the world of the progressives, women recite the *kaddish* prayer alongside the men.) Gradually, without awareness that my boundaries are shifting, I begin showing up earlier.

Looking down from my balcony perch, I see a rabbi cloak the bat mitzvah girl under the canopy of a wide *talis* and speak to her of her passions, her joys, her talents, her quests. Inside my bosom there is a surge of heat and sweet longing. In my day, a 13-year-old girl in an Orthodox family was not given a bat mitzvah or honored in any way. Secretly, I considered myself lucky to escape the onerous father-son preparation that was the lot of my older brother. But to my surprise, on this *shabbat* morning it dawns on me that, like the famished Esau returning from the wild, I am clamoring for an unclaimed blessing.

"May God continue to be with you just as he has always been with you from the moment of your birth," says the rabbi to the young girl entering womanhood. My father offered me an angst-drenched blessing as we gathered around the Sabbath table every Friday eve. He would spread his flattened palm over my head, his outstretched hand with balls of dark hair on each of his fingers, his fingernails cleaned but always jagged. I was a wayward plant, and my father beseeched God in a defeated tone to grow me up in the ways of the foremothers. *Ye'simech elohim* . . . I had no clear idea what it would mean to be righteous in the ways of Sarah, Rivka, Rachel and Leah, but I was quite sure it wasn't in the program. If anything, I would be righteous — or not — in my own unpredictable way, and this, I knew, was not likely to please God or my father, His unwavering emissary.

I forfeited my father's blessing, yet knew of no other that could do in its place. At the age of 18, I ventured out into the world with the swagger and fragility common to those who have lost the connection to their source. "May God continue to be with you just as he has always been with you from the moment of your birth." That Sabbath morning I risk leaning a little too far over the balcony edge, considering the matter from a whole new slant.

Hashiveinu ve'nashuva — return us and we will return. We sing those words as we return the Torah to the ark each *shabbat* morning. By showing up weekly in this place, I open myself to the possibility of "being returned" by some force that partakes of my personal history even as it presumably transcends it. What is this possibility that I allow to pierce my defenses? Some would say I am beginning to let go of that which separates me from *k'lal yisroel,* the community of Israel and its destiny. I have often heard that each of us must be willing to drop our story if we are to experience the sacred flow of life or the oneness of all being. The contrary may also be true. We have to intuit the profound truth of our personal story in order to find our rightful place in the larger narrative.

I have decided, in my first tentative act of return, to turn off the critical mind and let this be a purely visceral experience. At BJ, services are largely devoted to communal singing of ancient prayers in the original Hebrew; we are spared the haranguing or specious arguments that I associate with much of rabbinical discourse. Hardliners are known to criticize this place for its facile activation of feel-good circuitry in the brain, for its avoidance of onerous obligations. I don't mind the sweet laxity. In this context, judgment-free kindness is utterly seductive. Like so many other bruised seekers, I am being taken in, and the last thing I seek is a rational justification or too many obligations. For the first time since the rift, something inside is mercifully loosened.

As a freelance writer and a coach who works from home, I am usually exempt from most weekday dress codes. When I do go out, I indulge my own fashion sense with a certain joyful ease. Dressing for *shul* on *shabbos,* however, is a ritual with considerations all its own. Going way back to my earliest girlhood, it calls for conformity and originality, fitting in while standing out, creativity and diversity, an element of surprise within carefully delineated boundaries. Nowhere do the differences between the rigidity of then and the laxity of now show up more visually: These days, many, if not most, of the women at BJ wear slacks, some even come in jeans. Gone are the modest but well-cut dresses and tailored suits, the ruffled high-neck blouses, the obligatory nylons and above all, the stylish hats on the heads of the denizens of our stolidly bourgeois, Orthodox women's section. I have returned amid a new era of emancipation, but this new freedom does not help me to figure out who I want to be and how I want to dress, now that I am, once again, after so long a gap, and to a certain extent my own amusement, a regular "*shul*-goer."

When I open my closet and contemplate how to go about dressing each week, I expect to find my mother in the next room. As in the past, she is calling out to me not to "dawdle." Meanwhile, she is looking for two matching and runless thigh-high stockings to attach to her gartered girdle, a contraption I can just glimpse under her full-length slip. She is spraying Chanel No. 5, a light sweetness I like, and later, heavy mists of hairspray that I find suffocating. She is assembling her matching accessories: gloves, handkerchief, silk scarf, and most important, gingerly lifted from its box perched on high, the hat that will complement all the prior choices that have led up to its selection.

It has been said (by some wise folks who were definitely not rabbis) that clothes make the man. Since I know this to be even truer of woman, I have to give some thought to how it is I would like to appear each Saturday morning of the year. I contemplate my collection of quality but quirky clothes, many by obscure Parisian designers. I reflexively nod to what I remember as proper Sabbath garb — fabrics less body-hugging, skirts a tad longer, heels a little less spiked, necklines not so obviously suggestive. To simulate the special unburdened *shabbat* feeling that I knew in the distant past, I do not carry a purse, but rather find room for necessities in deep pockets if I can't leave them home. But I balk at trying to pretend I am someone who I am not. Coquetry comes naturally to me, and I'm not all that interested in hiding it.

Rather than get tangled up in all this, I've turned the Sabbath garb conundrum into a private game. I never plan my outfit ahead of time, never even give it a passing thought until I stand in front of my open closet. My self-styled prelude to prayer is putting together —

within ten minutes, a self-imposed time limit — an instant persona every week, with color and cut, trouser or skirt, formality or frivolity, always an improvised reflection of my mood and available resources. Surveying the results (the ten-minute time limit is strictly observed, otherwise this could go on forever), I amuse myself by remarking on which of my many selves is ready to make herself manifest for private musings and communal worship this week, hoping that she is in some subtle way different from whoever turned up the week before.

Before the end of the Sabbath morning service, E.T., my French Jewish art-dealer husband, often joins me in my balcony perch. He is a small-ish man, cuddly, rotund, with big brown eyes, a balding forehead, and dark hair that curls down past his collar. He likes to distinguish himself by sporting a black beret and wearing a red scarf. He never claps or sings or sways to the music as I do. His arms are often folded across his chest, his ruddy face inscrutable.

Saturday synagogue-going has never before been a feature or even a remotely considered option of E.T.'s life. In our two decades together in France, he would spend Saturdays combing antique markets, stocking up on gourmet specialties, conferring with colleagues in expensive galleries, occasionally indulging in a haircut and a man-icure at a snobbish establishment that has been grooming Parisian gentlemen for more than two hundreds years. With his errands done, E.T. regularly met with his bachelor-day friends for a late and leisurely lunch at which they exchanged social gossip and called the waiters by their first names in a comfortable bistro somewhere near the enclaves and boutiques frequented by a seasoned in-crowd. The scruffy balcony of the Saint Paul and Saint Andrews Methodist church where BJ is housed is an odd departure from familiar routines, yet along with me, the husband who followed me from France to the Upper West Side is becoming a *shabbat* morning regular.

When the service is over, E.T. dutifully takes it upon himself to go downstairs and, one by one, neatly store away the Bibles and prayer books that have been left in unruly heaps at the rear bookcases. E.T.

is a man accustomed to a certain order, a man with reverence for artifacts and books. Unlike me, he is also an extrovert. He has quickly and correctly concluded that the post at the rear bookcases downstairs is an excellent one for greeting and being greeted in turn.

Once, when I came down from the balcony after Sabbath services, a white-haired man was greeting E.T. and seizing the opportunity to exercise his stiffly literary French. The man had sympathetically concluded that we two newcomers had to be refugees from the recent rise in French anti-Semitism — a notion that took both of us by surprise. No, we responded, shaking our heads, it wasn't that, nothing so neat, nothing so classic motivated our return. How, then, to explain? We came here for personal reasons, to be near our college-age sons, because my elderly mother had suddenly become sick . . .

Then I thought to try out a word that is not French, but rather an expression dear to the *Mitteleuropa* from which so many of our Ashkenazi ancestors hail: *Sehnsucht*, soul sickness, or more precisely, the longing of the soul. It was not anti-Semitism that had inspired a leave-taking in our case; it was the essence of *Sehnsucht*.

I decided not to go there.

Spit, He Did Spit

I begin coming to Sabbath morning services earlier, arriving in time for the chanting of the Torah portion of the week. I often like to listen rather than read, inviting the sound of a phrase or sometimes a single word to jog my memory as to its narrative context.

One *shabbat* morning, a chanted phrase captures my attention. I hear *"ah na el na refah na la,"* please God, do heal her, the words from

"Yedid Nefesh," my harmonizing song with my father. I had forgotten that these words had a biblical source, and quickly open to the printed page to catch up with the story.

We are reading the story of Miriam in the Book of Numbers, Chapter 12. Miriam, Moses' older sister, speaks out of turn, expressing resentment of his exclusive leadership. God's anger flares up against her, and to show the uppity lady who's who, God smites her with skin-corroding leprosy.

Moses asks that his sister Miriam be forgiven for her thoughtless words and healed without further ado. *Ah na el na,* I beseech you, God, Moses prays with utmost brevity on Miriam's behalf, *refah na la,* please heal her. It is these words, Moses' prayer for Miriam, that found their way into *"Yedid Nefesh,"* the Sabbath song.

My pleasure in rediscovering the source quickly turns to horror. Moses asks for healing for his sister, and God responds, *Ve'aviha yarok, yarak be'paneha* — if her father had spit in her face — *haloh tikalem shivat yamim* — would she not be shamed for seven days? Miriam has misspoken, and her Heavenly Father has metaphorically spat in her face. Now she has the skin of a leper and must be excluded from the people of Israel for seven days before she can show her face and regain entry to their midst.

I look around me in the balcony: Is no one else alarmed by this almost casual reference to an apparently familiar custom of fathers spitting in their daughters' faces? Up here it is *shabbat* morning protocol as usual: the friends of the bar mitzvah boy are squirming with impatience, the loners are in their customary seats. I wonder who else is engaging with this text. Commentators agree that in the ancient Near East, spitting was among the most humiliating of disgraces, and it has long been considered a suitable response to the most reprehensible behavior. Miriam has spoken out of turn. Miriam has questioned Moses' judgment. Moses is a great and humble man, chosen by God. Miriam is rebuked for her criticism. God spits in her face just like a father would do. Miriam is clawing at her flaking skin.

Something inside me aches in a very personal way. Miriam was the dancing prophetess. It was she who, tambourine in hand, revealed to others the role of spirit incarnate when she led the fleeing daughters of Israel in celebratory rounds after they crossed the Red Sea. Miriam's dance was sacred woman's worship. It honored the banished goddess by incarnating disembodied words in female beauty, muscle and sinew. I remember myself as a lonely, misfit teenager, without guidance on the threshold to young womanhood and sadly out of step in a regimented Orthodox summer camp. A haunted and beautiful young woman named Shulamit taught me to whirl and to leap, to skip, to sway and to spiral. Like a nubile specter arising from the Song of Songs, she first taught me the ancient rhythms, and when she initiated me in the ways of Miriam, Shulamit helped me unite body and soul, inner and outer, and gifted me a lifelong expression.

Ve'aviha yarok, yarak . . . There is much in the Bible that we progressives would not consider admissible in today's make-nice world of manners, and a father spitting in a daughter's face is certainly one of those objectionable behaviors. Although the action is hypothetical ("if her father had spit"), the text repeats the verb for spit twice — *yarok, yarak,* spit, he did spit — thus assuring us this was to be no accidental ejection. After the spit comes his daughter's shame: Dad is aiming to demean. Is this the kind of projectile that's launched when the paternal rage button is pushed? Or is it calmly premeditated? Let the saliva rise like sap. Savor, swoosh, ready, take aim, and fire?

Sadly, this is not a form of censure that has grown out of style. As a shocked world recently witnessed when ultra-Orthodox men publicly spit on eight-year-old schoolgirls in a suburb of Jerusalem, it is a custom that has survived to our day.

Nausea rises in my own gut. In the world I fled, God and fathers who saw themselves as ambassadors for God were known to flip out and explode, sometimes predictably, often, terrifyingly, without warning. It was primarily my father's rage that had made me turn my back on a whole tradition. As a child, I was ill equipped (as children tend to be) to recognize an undiagnosed mood disorder in an adult who happened to be my parent, and therefore I had no way to anticipate, much less head off, these "episodes," as my mother used to helplessly call them. When I became pubescent, I could discern a clearer schema of cause and effect: The woman I was fated to be was the very energy that would ignite paternal rage. The syllogism was inescapable: If I persisted in being all that I was, there would be rage. My untenable fear was that it would either destroy me or defeat my inadvertent adversary.

There was no salvation other than flight; the only road to survival led to exile.

Now I am back, by way of some version of free choice with which I am still trying to come to terms. I sit up straighter, feeling my bones connect with the hard plank of the bench. I honor my courage for reentering these portals, for letting my eyes wash over the letters, for holding my ground.

I am too well steeped in the tradition not to know that there is much here that will assault my sensibilities, but I had not anticipated such a brute reminder of father-daughter tensions. What's more, I know that indifference to daughter abuse is but one of many offending biblical attitudes. The Torah tells us that homosexuality is an abomination, that a wife must be subservient to her husband, that a suspected adulteress must drink bitter waters, that not a single living creature is to be left alive in combat against certain of our enemies. There is something in the sacred text to ruffle just about everybody's feathers, if not to contest their essential human rights. What is it that keeps me from slamming this heavy book shut, stashing my reading glasses, and taking my leave?

A few weeks earlier I heard an iconoclastic rabbi named Art Green speak, with uncommon candor, at the Manhattan JCC. He asked why, and whether, we must still bother with this archaic tradition, filled as it is with outworn attitudes, ritualized minutia, and offensive pronouncements. Rabbi Green admitted his aversion to much of the "obsessive-compulsive in Jewish observance," and also confessed his doubts as to the "truth contents of a frozen-in-time revelation at Sinai." He questioned, as I long have, much of what we have come to understand about God from the biblical narrative. Why read this ancient book aloud for all to hear every week? What are we seeking here that will leave us better off than we would be without the Torah's teachings?

Rabbi Green (who likes to be called Art) did not offer a definitive reply, but he did encourage us to keep raising questions, because raising questions that shake up the status quo is what Jews do best. Art reminded us that even though Jews have never been more than a tiny percentage of the globe's population, we have nonetheless enriched human history with some paradigm-changing insights and values. There must be something in our heritage that creates favorable conditions for introspection and innovation. Like the BJ rabbis and other contemporary, progressive Jewish teachers, Art asks us to keep diving for pearls, to hold fast to the possibility that Judaism and the God of its covenant have a built-in capacity for reciprocal evolution.

Now in his 70s, Art has been in the avant-garde of religious thought since the 1960s and has contributed several notable books, including *Seek My Face, Speak My Name*, which pursues this concept of human and theological evolution. He urges us to invest our own hearts and minds in the proposition that Judaism can again be part of a crucial paradigm shift — for he believes that nothing less than the viability of human life on our planet is at stake.

There was a time in my life when I turned my back on all this, not without good reason. It cannot be a facile decision to feel my way back in, to reconsider the covenant, to imagine, collectively with both seekers and doubters, what it might mean for us as Jews, ambivalent in our loyalty to a complex past, to champion our own evolution and play a crucial role in humanity's future. It is for the sake of these larger issues that I struggle to overcome my own emotional limitations.

Ah na el na refah na la — Please God, do heal her and show to her Your face. Who, indeed, will heal the festering wounds of a dancing woman whose father has publicly repudiated her? How to heal the scaling face of one whose father wished her to be shamed? How to evolve from one scorned to one who joins others in lighting the way?

My Father's Eyes

I'd spotted Joseph before I started to go to BJ, but back then he was just another scrawny guy in an oversized jacket trying to look occupied, walking the streets, resting on random benches, occasionally talking to himself while sorting through trash. Once or twice I glimpsed him asleep on the upstairs couch at Starbucks, his scruffy shopping bags full. Even there, he was unobtrusive, retaining a certain dignity all his own. With his thick glasses and depressed mouth, peaked nose, and thinning hair, Joseph is part of the Upper West Side neighborhood scene, visible to some, invisible to most. Many cross paths with him every day, but I am the only one who knows that he has my father's eyes.

At BJ, Joseph has a permanent seat in the front row, and in my first years, there was not a single event at which he was not at his post. He is often on his feet, raised by an irrepressible enthusiasm. Attentive though he is, towards the end of a long service he inevitably gets a little restless. In the blink of an eye, as if he could fly, he is suddenly in the balcony, first in the front row, then, like some private detective, checking things out behind the rear seats. Before I can make eye contact, he vanishes, only to reappear downstairs, front row center, reclaiming the only real home he has.

It's a good thing he's there, too. Whenever one of the rabbis needs a little help as to where in the text an unusual use of some word might be found, they look to Joseph. He never fails to reply, without a trace of self-importance. What's more, Joseph sings the loudest and holds notes the longest of anyone in BJ, a synagogue well known for its enthusiastic vocals. His whoops and flourishes are exuberant expressions of his unwavering love for God. Once, when my older brother came to visit, he noticed it, too: Joseph sings the way my dad did when he was on the crest of his manic mood swings, and Joseph, too, sings for a God who hasn't singled him out for any special favors.

Joseph is always neatly dressed in clothes that are a few sizes too big for his slight frame. His face reminds me of a bird who has been ejected from the nest. He pads around with a light gait, noiseless in gum-soled shoes. He has large square glasses with thick watery lenses, and behind those thick lenses are the same big, sea-green eyes my father had, his also hidden behind glass. (One day someone told me my eyes changed colors, from yellow to green to brown, and at that time it made me proud, for it was just one more way I took after my dad. When I mentioned it to my father, however, he seemed confused. I learned then that my dad was so preoccupied with the big questions, he didn't know the color of his own eyes.)

Although I am still shy about making contact with the others, once or twice I deliberately catch Joseph's eye just long enough for him to know I am approachable. Soon enough, he is regularly rushing towards me after services, speaking rapid-fire, with great urgency. There is no preamble; in his private universe we have already been together for hours wrangling over a fine point. "That's it, Rabbi So-and-So, he's the one who knew to look at the question from another angle, the angle of the yet unborn, because as you know, it says in the Mishnah . . ."

On and on — he's got volumes stored in his brain — sacred texts are served up as fodder for the agitated gristmill of the mind. Joseph wrestles with the text in a feverish effort to figure out what it is God really wants and needs from us. This is no trifling matter. God's plan is, of course, unknowable, yet it is only through hard-won clarity that this imperiled world might be saved.

Our conversations wring me out.

He will evoke a word or a phrase that I haven't heard since childhood. He will tussle with it, suck hungrily at the marrow, then ask me if I agree with the meaning he extracts. I don't always get it. He is not skilled at hiding his impatience, though he is always kind. If only I would realize the urgency, the importance, so much time has passed, so many minds have labored and yet . . . and still . . .

"Joseph," I once said in an effort to soothe him, "it's all right. God loves you. No matter what."

With that, Joseph excused himself and disappeared.

After nearly forty years of estrangement from synagogue life, the BJ habit has swelled from a seventy-five-minute Friday-night fix to an additional two hours on Saturday morning and, quite frequently, at least one additional weekday activity, be it serving dinner at the congregation's homeless shelter, paying a stranger a condolence call, listening to a visiting scholar, or taking a weekday lunch-hour to attend the Talmud class in midtown. I am beginning to make new friends and reconnect in a relaxed way with a few familiar faces. On average, each week, I have at least one coffee or lunch or dinner with an acquaintance from BJ. Still, I am holding back from full acknowledgment of my religious, social, and political engagement with this place.

Affiliation with the BJ community reintroduces a fundamental childhood rhythm, long forsaken, into my life. Life takes place over six days slung between the anchoring posts of a preceding and a culminating Sabbath. I look forward to the pause in dailyness, to the otherworldly majesty and soulful sweetness that our spiritual mentor, Abraham Joshua Heschel, describes as a "window on eternity." I begin setting out a few *shabbat* guidelines for myself, and even if sometimes they are honored more in the breach than in the practice, they remain spiritual goals. I will not take public transportation on the Sabbath or eat in a restaurant. I will not conduct any business transactions or burden my thoughts with future plans. I do my best (and too often fail) to avoid checking e-mail or using the Internet. Instead, I set aside time for reading, walking along the river, and conversing with friends. I soon join an all-woman's study group in which we read the biblical commentary of a singular woman scholar named Avivah Zornberg, who relishes teasing out the role of the unconscious in these ancient texts. I indulge in afternoon naps that invite my own unconscious to visit me with deeply reassuring scenes of reconciliation with figures from my religious past.

Nevertheless, I can't bring myself to self-identify as a regular synagogue-goer. If pressed, I will admit to my involvement in this particular organization, always rushing to explain how BJ is different from a mainstream community: The distribution of roles is guided by a post-gender sensibility, no one is grilled about their beliefs, non-Jews are welcomed in the mix. This is a non-judgmental, inclusive, socially-conscious version of my Jewish past that sings the same songs while offering a wide array of choices as to how each one of us wants to nurture his or her spiritual growth.

BJ also provides an outlet for my under-exercised social conscience. Throughout the Bush years and into the Obama renewal of hope, this congregation is results-oriented in its progressive politics. I am drawn to the opportunity to sit and talk with the homeless women who spend weeknights in the synagogue basement, so I volunteer once monthly to set up their dinner. I join the struggle for better conditions for local restaurant workers, and by boycotting designated establishments, we achieve our reforms. I add my name to the committee that looks after the bereaved in a gesture of gratitude for the support I received when mourning the death of my own mother. These things I do, but always with a few disclaimers.

My denials go on and on. Even as I note that BJ activities are taking up more space in my calendar, I do not accord them any special status. BJ is simply one of the many things I do in the course of my new, exciting, self-styled New York life. My extroverted husband enjoys the communal aspect of BJ, as a place to gather each week and converse with increasingly familiar faces. The music is undeniably uplifting, and the return to text is enriching. Still, I consider myself an ambivalent member in deliberation over degrees of commitment. I am not open to acknowledging a deeper level of attraction; I cannot yet frankly entertain anything like a need to reconcile with my parents, or a hunger for some spiritual truths, or a tug towards a renewed loyalty to historical peoplehood. I carefully avoid conversations that might ask me to pronounce my opinions as to the truth content of Jewish tradition. I do not want to be interrogated or pinned down.

The mirror in the downstairs ladies room reflects my face with its deeper grooves and sagging jaw lines. Could it be that I have simply come full circle? Some have suggested this trajectory is so classical as to be ennobling. I fear that it might be trite. Then again, surely there is nothing shameful about enacting the universal pattern of rupture and return. T. S. Eliot famously summed it up: "The end of our exploring will be to arrive where we started and to know the place for the first time." Why persist in denial? There is something deeply soothing about returning to the site of the original wound and finding healing energy right there on site.

I'd like to deny another truth, but at the end of the day, resistance is futile: As I grow closer to mortality, I increasingly seek solace in the spiritually transcendent. I want to feel part of something that was there before I came on the scene and will persist long after I am gone.

There remains one bottom line I am not ready to sign. I will not renounce youthful rebellion, even when viewed from the sobered perspective of age. This is not a matter of repentance or repudiation of my choices in the past. The Jewish tradition offered me little in the breakaway heyday of my youth, and I will not betray that youthful self, the raw courage she showed and the price of loneliness she paid for severing ties. *Lech lecha,* or more precisely, *lechi lach:* you go forth, girl. Leaving home without parental sponsorship is the sine qua non of any autonomous spiritual journey, and my younger self cut herself loose and ventured forth. She is a young woman I wish to champion, defend, and even protect. The question becomes: Can I re-embrace a tradition without losing myself, betraying her, or discrediting my life's arc?

Then again, what would it bring me if I loosened my attachment to my own story? I am willing to wager, or at least entertain the possibility, that I might reclaim more of myself by walking through this door than I would by stubbornly passing it by.

On one Friday night in early winter, I skip BJ services to join a friend at the New York City Ballet. When the performance ends, I look forward to my half-hour walk home. I have some important matters to go through in my mind, and nothing is more conducive to the sorting than a brisk walk through the city after dark.

Shortly after my return from France in 2001, I embarked on a new career path. Within two years, I completed my training and certification as a life coach. Despite the upheavals of 9/11 and the unexpected death of my mother, this was a fertile and hopeful time for me.

Fast-forward to 2008 and I am losing my footing in this rapidly deteriorating economic climate. I was hoping to get a well-paid coaching gig in the corporate world, but now the plans are, as they like to say in these darkening days, "on hold." I need to figure out other sources of income as well as to grapple with the bigger questions: Whom do I want to coach, what do I have to offer, and how will I convince them to pay for my services?

I'm no stranger to disappointment along the career path, and suspending my own rule against planning ahead on the Sabbath, I'm looking forward to strolling alone through the misty city and sorting it all out. But I haven't gone more than one block when I run straight into Joseph, who appears out of the fog like a shade, lugging a big paper bag. I'm surprised to see him this far downtown, near Lincoln Center, a good twenty blocks out of our usual territory, at nearly 11 o'clock on a Friday night. He greets me with a whooping "Good *shabbos*." Luckily, he is headed downtown and I am walking up, meaning we will exchange greetings and I will walk on in heavenly solitude.

No such luck. He insists on gallantry, on turning around and escorting me the twenty city blocks uptown, all the way home.

"Joseph," I ask him, "What's in that bag you're carrying? It looks so heavy."

"*Sefarim*," he answers, meaning sacred books.

"But Joseph, why are you carrying them around with you tonight?"

He tells me he is on his way to Columbus Circle, where he will study with some mystery man at midnight. I nod. He tells me we will be better off walking on West End Avenue, away from the Broadway crowds, and I am not about to argue. I am tempted to pin him down. Perhaps if I am intrusive, he will fly away.

"Joseph, where did you learn?" I ask.

"Brooklyn."

"Joseph, where do you live?"

"Uptown."

That's all the information I'm going to get. Then it's his turn to ask me a question.

"What's your Hebrew name?"

Now, that's a whole other story, my not really having been given a Hebrew name, but only a Yiddish one — a story I don't feel like going into. "My Hebrew name is Yiddish, Shayne Perele, it's after my father's mother, that's my name."

That's all it takes: Joseph is off and running. "Shayne Perele, listen," he calls out, launching into his tortured harangue as he trots by my side. "Shayne Perele, were you there when they said . . . did you hear . . . do you think . . . do you know . . . what about this teaching, Shayne Perele, and that one . . ."

I keep walking faster, determined to get home before a tension headache sets in. As children, we were always told that our lives came with a mission attached, that it was our task to discern the mission and to fulfill it, and that our names would likely give us a clue as to the nature of our special calling. My name, Shayne Perele, beautiful pearl, was embarrassing and a total non-starter. All I could think of was that like a pearl, I was formed as a result of so many irritants.

The fog hides all others from view, and Joseph is the irritant. When finally we get to my corner, I stop to wish him good night.

He faces me squarely. "Shayne Perele." No one but my father has repeatedly called me by that name. The daughter he would lament as his undoing was the namesake of the mother he always loved.

"Shayne Perele," Joseph repeats. My annoyance is steadily mounting, but I am riveted to this apparition in the fog.

"Shayne Perele, it is for your sake that I learn, you have the *zichut*, the merit."

"Joseph, I have no merit. None whatsoever."

"No, really, if it were not for you, I would not have had this chance — to recite Torah, to learn . . ."

In the lunchtime Talmud class, we learned that forefather Jacob's blessing of his son Joseph forever protects Joseph from the evil eye. On this night, I run away, as I always have. I run away and I pray that God, whose ways are unknowable, will bless Joseph and keep those eyes forever from harm.

To Rise Above Wrath

I'm annoyed with my husband because of the sweater he's chosen to wear to BJ this early winter Saturday morning. E.T. walks West End Avenue coatless, sporting the sweater, circa 1972, for all to see and, he imagines, to unconditionally admire. This sweater evokes in him feelings of pride, connection, safety, reliability, belonging. He starts to tell me for maybe the fifteenth time how long he's managed to keep it, how carefully he's preserved it, how excellent is the quality of the wool which is special and sheared and found only in the top Austrian and Swiss ski clothiers. The more he holds forth on the merits of this sweater, the greater my irritation grows. The sweater barely fits around a stomach that has gained considerable rotundity since the garment's acquisition some four decades back. It's made of a thick wool felt, cranberry colored with black trim, and it sports a sort of unapologetic Tyrolian gloom. That particular shade of bluish red has a depressing way of darkening circles under the eyes and giving the face a sallow tint. But worst of all, as far as I am concerned, is all the mental stagnation the cloth tightly weaves in.

The sweater was a gift from his mother way back when. However unflattering the color, however tight the circumference, he's going to trot it out annually and make of this humble garment a whole life lesson. It's about continuity and care and all those increasingly unfashionable European values. It's about loyalty and sturdiness and the appreciation of quality. It's a proud statement of not subscribing to the easy-disposability ethic with which we are daily confronted over here in the savage New World, where I have relentlessly pressured him to make a home. So whether I like it or not, he's not only going to wear the sweater, he's going to make of it a *cause célèbre*. What's more, he's going to scoff at me, and not in a very nice way, should I choose not to champion this sweater for its durability, its service, and most of all, its provenance in the glorious past.

I feel my blood boiling with something approaching rage. As it is a Sabbath morning and we are now mounting the steps to the BJ balcony, I resort to a meditation technique: breathe in and out and just observe sensation. Don't buy in, don't tell a whole story, don't lash out, just be present with whatever arises. We take our seats on the aisle of the upstairs balcony, me trying to fathom what is bringing up so much anger this particular weekend. In the case of the sweater, I know it has to do with my resentment of my husband's attachment to his past. I am convinced that our lives would be so much richer (in every way) if he could simply let go of some of these attachments and approach life with unfettered energy. His refusal to do so is symbolized by a too-tight, boiled-felt sweater, and I am in no mood for facile forgiveness.

I keep on breathing, singing along a little halfheartedly with the prayers. Then suddenly I see clearly and relax into sheer remorse. How can I be so peeved at my husband for his attachment to his past, even if it has to express itself in the flaunting of an offending sweater, when here I am, after a forty-or-so-year hiatus, doing a pretty good imitation of what my parents did every Saturday morning of their lives? Were it not for my attachment to the past, were it not for my cherishing of their gifts, wouldn't I be in Pilates class or walking along the river or home writing an e-mail or out to brunch with a friend? Were it not for all those ties that bind, all those ties I have expended so much furious energy to unbind, wouldn't we all be somewhere else on this brisk and bright beckoning day?

"Psst, E.T., listen, okay, I'm sorry I got so sore about the sweater."

E.T. is absorbed in reading the Bible chapter of the week, a practice I know he finds useful for his work as an art dealer and enriching in his role of extrovert with general culture. I lean over again and whisper loudly, "I mean, it's okay, you know, how you feel about the sweater and everything like that."

He peers at me over his reading glasses, shaking his head, wondering what it is I'm mumbling about now.

*I can't deny that I'm having anger issues lately, and coming to the syna-*gogue is exacerbating them. Just the night before, during Friday-night services, I almost really lost it. I arrived midway, really inexcusably late, when the congregation was already on its feet amid the silent reading of the *Shmoneh Esrei*. I have known since childhood that this is an un-voiced prayer, recited standing with feet close together rooted to a spot, which is embellished with a certain amount of choreographed bowing in various directions and heel-lifting at punctual times. The entire balcony is standing, awaiting the conclusion of this important prayer, an end that is signaled by the cantor beginning to hum a soulful tune. The *nigun* (melody) is sounded, and all around people relax their stance.

Spotting two available seats high up in a pew across the aisle, I politely excuse myself and try to slide by the man in front of me. He whirls on me in silent outrage. His accusing look says, *What is wrong with you? Can't you wait until the end of the prayer?* I am quite sure I had, but then again, perhaps I had not taken the trouble to notice that he, out of step with the others, had not quite finished. If so, that was an oversight on my part, but by turning on me in irate censure he is pushing a few rage buttons that so far have not been triggered in these parts. Wary of an unrestrained outburst — I simply have zero tolerance for being harshly rebuked by unshaven men wrapped in prayer shawls — I stare at him in ill-concealed fury.

My children tell me I am scary looking in those moments, and for all I know this may be so. But the man will not let me pass. First he does his concluding three steps backwards, bows to the left and to the right and to the front, then after a few moments, comes forward three steps and lifts his heels to Heaven, before closing his prayer book and kissing it. Then he turns to me with patronizing indulgence. Looking down at me in my inadequacy, he wants to explain to me all about the *Shmoneh Esrei,* what it means and why I should not have interrupted him during its silent reading.

By now I am aggressively moving past him, turning around only to hiss with maximum venom — *"You, whoever you are, have nothing to teach me that I don't already know"* — before making my infuriated way to the coveted seats.

Usually, lighting the Sabbath candles, sipping the wine, biting into a fresh challah go a long way toward soothing my agitation. This week, I am unappeased. Hours later, as I finally drift off to sleep, I still feel the stabs of my anger.

I volunteer to facilitate a **Rosh** Chodesh *(New Moon) gathering of* BJ women. I explain to the woman who runs the monthly sessions my general interest in the topic of women and visibility. (As a newly certified life coach, I have founded a program for women known as the Visibility Project.) In this context, I will speak of women's affinity with the moon: Like the moon we all go through phases of relative invisibility and visibility. There are times when we are seen and appreciated by others for who we are. There are also times when we are unnoticed + unacknowledged + excluded = invisible.

The organizer agrees that I may lead a session. On this particular Saturday, my BJ habit has extended beyond the morning service into a *shabbos* afternoon activity. With its cohort of women, this gathering reminds me of how I would spend every *shabbos* afternoon with my observant neighborhood girlfriends throughout my childhood. In the half-light of the church basement, sitting in a big circle of flimsy folding chairs, we grown-up women gather this wintry afternoon, and I introduce the afternoon's theme.

As a group we agree that, like the moon, although less predictably, we women move along a spectrum between invisibility and full manifestation. My invitation to explore the merits and drawbacks of each phase leads to a lively discussion. Some say that invisibility, irksome though it often is, can offer women relief from living up to others' standards. I offer that Virginia Woolf once said, "The eyes of others are our prisons," and ask for their comments. One or two women speak of the restfulness granted by the times in our lives when we are not seen. Someone else counters that imposed invisibility is a grievous affront to our gender. I suggest that we can hold all these to be true: both visibility and invisibility have positive points and drawbacks. I do not see it as a choice. Rather, like the moon, we can temporarily vanish, only to recreate ourselves in burgeoning degrees of wholeness.

I edge toward the provocative. In our tradition, God is pretty clear that He will not be glimpsed, that we are to trust in the non-manifest. Graven images, not to mention golden calves, are forbidden. So be it: We are not to see God in any visual representation. The disturbing question is the degree to which Divine consciousness can or cannot be said to see us.

The Rabbis are notorious for the awful ways they view women. (It is good to remember that the Rabbis are not God, even if they are self-appointed conduits for Divine wisdom and the shapers of the many laws that govern traditional Jewish life.) The Rabbis do not hesitate to assert that women are troublemakers, idle gossips, frivolous yet dangerous distractions from the right path. Women, according to the Talmud, are conceived not only in procreative sin, but in a blood stain. Our essence is impurity, impurity is our essence. We all know there is a gaping discrepancy between how we as women view ourselves and how we have long been seen by Jewish authorities.

It's a delicate subject, to be sure. It is easy enough to feel angry and alienated. We end the session agreeing that BJ does much to heal the primal pain. That is why we women are drawn to this place. Here, women study, pray, teach, and come up to the Torah side by side with men. But does that mean we have carved out the path, or even found the language, to articulate our journey from the sullied margins to the communal mix? Does it mean we know how to heal the accumulated exclusion and forgive the slander of the past? In my heart, I think no, not fully, not all of it, not all of us, not yet. Judith Plaskow, whose book *Standing Again at Sinai: Judaism from a Feminist Perspective* made a huge impact in 1990, was recently quoted as saying, "Everything has changed and nothing has changed." Millennia of embedded sexism are not wiped out in a few decades of new policy and halting good will. Yet we nonetheless experience an opening, a loosening of old fixations, a quickening of interest in a new idea.

After leading the lively exchange about women and visibility for the women's *Rosh Chodesh* group, I receive appreciative feedback from the participants. One week later, thinking it natural, I ask the organizer if I might not lead a few more workshops for women. *Hineni*, I'm here and ready to make a contribution. "When we need you, we will let you know," says she as she hastily makes her way through the hungry crowd gathered for a reception at the conclusion of Sabbath morning prayers. The message is clear, or so it seems to me at the time: *What makes you think you can gain membership in this club? You've been away far too long.*

I am just as reactive sensing rejection by Jewish women as I am suspecting censure from Jewish men. This time it's a woman rabbi who has pushed all the wrong buttons. Gathering storm clouds urge me to bolt from this basement and nurse my hurt feelings at home.

When Judaism as a contact sport gets a little rough, I rummage through my repository of inspiring dictums. *Hey, Suzi, just take it lightly* . . . the words of a woman about to depart from this life echo in my mind. They try to pry open a whole dimension of possibility in this moment of hurt, but something inside contracts from the sting.

I am walking fast towards the exit, figuring I need to go home and just get a handle on all that's bursting at the seams, when I nearly bump straight into Joseph. He looks at me with those sea-green eyes from behind his thick glasses and blocks my exit.

"Shayne Perele, always on the run."

I say nothing.

"So what do you have, an appointment somewhere?"

There can be no use explaining my agitation to him.

"Yeah, really? You're in such a rush?"

I mumble something not very convincing.

"Come have something to eat before it's all gone."

I stop for a moment and take the measure of this man. He's making steady eye contact and smiling at me and slowly shaking his head. He is telling me, and for once without words, that in this world, even if better that I shouldn't know from it, there are many slings and arrows. Surreptitiously he lets me see the top of the small whiskey flask he carries around in his oversized pocket. He has an extra paper cup and I agree to take a swig. The whiskey burns and takes the edge off my anger. I'm beginning to get it. Running away might work sometimes, but it is not the only solution. I look at Joseph and have to admit that in spite of everything, he is able in his own way to hold his ground. I get tossed, insulted, and agitated, while he never ascribes blame.

I nod into those sea-green eyes, watery now behind those glasses. Then I thank Joseph, for in a flash I recognize he is savvy, far more savvy than I, in the ways of survival. I turn around, grab a small paper plate, and follow him to the nearly decimated buffet table. We are happy for the ravaged remains of chopped egg and a few bites of tuna salad.

Peace unto thee, angels of peace, angels of on high, bless me with your peace.

This is the evening it erupts. I come home from the BJ Friday-night services in an altered state. The gathering ended with the singing of *"Shalom Aleichem,"* a song welcoming the angels, bestowing upon us a heavenly blessing as we come and go on our earthly rounds, a blessing offered by angels as they make their winged way between realms. This song is an invocation, one that inaugurated our family's ingathering at the *shabbat* table every Friday night of my childhood. It was a song that marked a profound shift — from anxiety to serenity, from divisiveness to unity, from grudge to absolution, from displeasure to gratitude. It was an anthem of one family reconnecting with itself and infusing the entire world with Sabbath love. Exceptionally, BJ is singing *"Shalom Aleichem"* in the tune we always sang together as a family. My eyes close of their own volition, and I am carried back by a thousand voices to the Beforetime, the time before rupture was even so much as a ripple in the unruffled child-mind. This is Jewish grace, the way a song and its imagery illuminate a pathway to abiding peace. I once knew this place so intimately — its aroma of challah bread, the imprint of sweet wine on the tongue, the anticipation of chicken stewing in its juices, how the room would waver if you looked directly through the glow of the candles' flame. And I still know how to follow the simple lulling melody to a sacred still point.

Back in France, I had tried to teach *"Shalom Aleichem"* to my children when they were growing up, but perhaps I did so only half-heartedly, perhaps the song was attenuated by my inner doubts, my loneliness, my loss. But this evening I would come home with the Sabbath song of angels renewed in my heart. I would teach the song again to my *bechor*, my first-born Raphael who had just days ago returned from far-off places; once again we two, he and I, we will bond in tenderness and complicity, as in days of yore.

But Raphael, a professional percussionist, is already deep into drum practice. I feel the resounding vibration the instant I step through the front door. At the age of 26, he has boomeranged back into our midst after spending six months in the home of his tabla guru in Calcutta, and for him there is no such entity as the Jewish Sabbath. He has sequestered himself in the far bathroom, switching from tabla to the long-neglected congas in whose far more aggressive rhythms he was adept before going to Asia. Even muffled by a towel, the airwaves reverberate with mounting passion. I imagine a stench of sweat and rising testosterone, and I am assaulted by warrior sounds of foreign tribes arising from the dark continent, while I had so much wanted us to ingather our own lost tribe and come together in the Sabbath light. His rhythmic thunder pulverizes my puny, pleading song of the angels into dust. I have no air to breathe, no more present-moment mind, only this pounding from the room and from inside my head, a pounding that reduces all my resolve to rubble.

This New York City apartment is not the family home back in France. It is a room of my own, so to speak, a sanctuary to which I retreated after putting in my time as Mom. My love for Raphael is as fierce as anything I have ever known, but I was not prepared for his landing back in the middle of my hard-won space. I am also, though less obviously, irked that neither E.T. nor I can subsidize rent for our kid in another place just now. After six months of devotion to music without an income, Raphael's money woes have landed him in a similar bind.

I am not prepared for my Sabbath longing to clash with his resurrecting, percussive passion. But here we are, on a Friday night that belongs to each of us in wholly different ways, all collapsing into the same weak center, all wishing we could do better, all wishing we had a room of our own far away from here. I rap angrily on the bathroom door, calling out that he stop playing — and right now, too.

I have pushed his rage button. It's a high-voltage charge that passes from me to him. He comes out with a sweaty brow and naked torso, his eyes red-rimmed with fatigue and clouded with resentment. Or is it hatred? Or is it extreme frustration at being thwarted and mis-understood? I suspect it is rage at his own failure to progress towards independence, as though I were the primary obstacle to his self-real-ization. Why have I allowed myself to assume that dangerous role, to become the screen onto which someone else projects their inner rage? I like to think that we in this household are more self-aware and highly evolved, but it turns out that in extremis, we are not.

E.T., who saunters in to announce our waiting dinner, has to separate mother and son after a volley of shouting, cursing, and door slamming. The two of us are broken and soiled, drained of life force, and profoundly disappointed, mostly in ourselves. It is in this sorry state that I have to make my way back to the Sabbath table and do what I can to get through the meal.

*Even though Raphael's rage is lately directed at me, I have to under-*stand it because it also lives (and originates?) in me. Like an internal tsunami, it does not come often, but when, without warning, rage overtakes and subsumes, it washes away all my bearings.

Maybe I should carry a "Warning: Contents Explosive" sign. I want to be the wise mother, I want to be Chochma, Universal Wisdom Herself, but I am much closer to an inchoate Fury. I can do no right: I am maligned on the one hand as the unwelcoming, self-absorbed sourpuss of a mom; I am resented on the other hand for anything I do that seems motherly-meddlesome. I have been spending many quiet hours at home, writing, reflecting, and planning some new entrepreneurial capers. Allegedly, it is selfish and unsupportive of me not to tolerate Raphael's percussion in the next room, especially when he temporarily has no other place to go. When I discuss the future — his, that is — whether in personal or professional terms, he is revolted by my "maternal angst." I feel criticized, and I'm not good at processing that. Having been trained and maimed in the early fight for psychic survival, I live under the Scorpio sign, given to retaliatory extravagance when attacked, spurned, encroached upon, or censured — especially when I imagine I am being unfairly accused. (I feel so profoundly, so abidingly accused.)

There are stretches of time when I maintain an even keel. I have been a student of yoga and meditation for over twenty years. Still, when piqued, I am overtaken with a rage that sometimes shatters its fragile vessel. Raphael has been a far more devoted student of *vipassana* meditation than I. He has sat for several ten-day courses in complete silence, afterwards meditating at least one hour each day. This is his campaign against inheriting my toxicity. But whatever it is that informs and infuses my anger, it will not be meditated out of existence or pulled up by the roots. It is not so easily, and certainly not permanently, appeased.

Although it is late winter and the Northeast is still windy and cold, I accept the offer of an overnight stay at a friend's vacant house on Fire Island. There will be walks on the beach and sea winds to salt-spray the eyes. The sunrise on the horizon will bring another perspective on petty woes. I will stoke the firewood in the stove and recalibrate my internal rhythms.

To my delight, Raphael accepts my invitation to come join me. We arrive after dark and head straight for the beach. Clouds hover around the half moon, but for the moment it glistens unobstructed in the sky. The tide is rushing in, and my sweatshirt does not offer me enough warmth against the cold air. Raphael and I decide to walk faster to generate body heat. I like the iodized aroma of seaweed, the spray of mist in my face, the way the damp sand feels between my bravely exposed toes.

We can hardly see where we are going in the thickening dark under a starless sky. The waves rise and softly roar before they break hard and rush to the shore. As I look out on the churning white caps, I feel inhabited by another presence. I tug at Raphael to get him to sit next to me on a big rock overlooking the sea.

I tell him again how my father, who died of a heart attack suddenly one night when Raphie was only 4, was a stridently Orthodox Jew, a stop-at-nothing crusader for the cause. His was a way of life based on the Absolute Truth of revelation, as handed down by God to the chosen on Sinai and frozen in time.

Interestingly, my father considered himself a well-reasoned moderate: Our Orthodoxy accommodated modernity in many ways. I was offered a high-quality education in a preppy Manhattan day school sufficiently forward-looking to discontinue the stenography track for girls and integrate us into Talmud class instead. My mother did not shave her head, and on hot summer days no one objected to our wearing shorts and sleeveless shirts while frolicking in our Catskill bungalow colony. Our first allegiance was to Jewish content and continuity, with allegiance to America, the country of religious freedom, coming in a close second. As long as we kept strictly kosher, said our daily prayers, observed the Sabbath and holidays, devoted ourselves to our Hebrew studies, stayed chaste, married within the Orthodox world, and lived in a homogenous community within walking distance of an Orthodox synagogue, all would be well. I was slated to go to a city college, major in education, and be a schoolteacher like my mom. This would permit me a seemly quota of modest self-expression along with enough pocket money to afford little extras within a circumscribed world. The prescribed way of life would allow enough time for me to properly mother my own children and prepare chicken soup and potato kugel for *shabbos* meals. We had only to follow a middle-of-the-road path of pious conformity, remain modest and unassuming in our ways, and all would be well.

Somehow, my father's only daughter, Shayne Perele, named for his saintly mother, couldn't get with the program. My idolatrous worship of beauty for its own sake, my passion for dance, my curiosity about other cultures, my sensual attunement to the flesh, and my attraction to all that was taboo made it impossible for me to live within the drawn lines. I've often explained to my son how my own explosive life-energy combusted with the social upheaval of the late '60s and '70s to turn me into a full-blown rebel. I was younger than Raphie is now when I forfeited all sense of meaning in this life, according to my father, and along with that my passport to the World-To-Come. My coming-of-age as a non-adherent to the plan was an outcome to which Dad could not surrender with equanimity or grace.

I defied yet feared God's wrath, along with my father's, since the two to me were one and the same. I had to develop some mighty anger energy of my own if I was to escape unscathed from either or both.

There are some details I've never chosen to share with my son, though the two of us have always been open and complicit. There are scenes that the good mother in me thought best to spare him. I am thinking of the night of my father's first heart attack when he was in his mid-50s and I was 17. It is early June, nearing the end of my senior year at the prestigious Ramaz School in Manhattan. Lilah and I are already well launched in our explorations of life beyond the pale. We have eaten non-kosher food, we have hitchhiked on the Sabbath, we have petted heavily with irreligious young men. By then my father knows that come graduation, I will do whatever I can to find lodging outside of his home, maybe even defy his prohibition against residency in the fiendishly godless playground known as out-of-town college. He has insisted that I apply only to a CUNY college and attend class from home; surreptitiously I am exploring other options, prepared even to get a job as a waitress, join the hippy movement, and find my own place in Manhattan. These are days when the world is cracking open for my generation, and my dad is twisting himself into knots trying to make sure I don't leave his malodorous home. Lately the tension between us is such that he feels incapacitated and spends most of his time in his room. Even though the weather is fine, he never leaves the house, invoking failing health, except to go to the nearby Young Israel on *shabbos*.

My dad's heartache at my anticipated parting is so severe that it translates into palpable chest pains. Doctors assure him these are stress attacks. I am under relentless parental pressure to abandon my rebellious course, a mutiny that all agree is the cause of my father's not-so-mysterious pain.

One evening in June, at the end of my senior year of high school, I am in my room playing a Bob Dylan album, listening to him sing one stanza over and over again: *Come mothers and fathers throughout the land and don't criticize what you can't understand. Your sons and your daughters are beyond your command* . . . Could it be that beyond this suffocating house there awaits a whole world of free-thinking people who share my feelings of alienation from my parents? *Your old road is rapidly agin'.* Why doesn't my father accept that his God-and-Torah trip is on its way out? His chest pains must be getting worse as my mother is hovering over his bed, then making anxious phone calls. Why can't he just relax and let me be? *Please get out of the new one, if you can't lend a hand.* He should live his life the way he's chosen to and give me the right to live mine. I'm wondering what would happen if I just took a subway into Manhattan and then roamed around the East Village. Maybe I could hook arms with someone the way Dylan's girl Suze does with him on the cover of that *Freewheeling* album I'm going to listen to next.

My father says that if I leave home he will never show his face in the community again. He thunders that I bring him nothing but shame. But in the world beyond this religious tyranny, I might learn to stroll through life in a whole new way. I might even get invited to one of those folk music clubs, where I wouldn't tell anyone about the life I left behind. Those people who gather to sing about freedom in all its forms could not be expected to begin to comprehend my freakish background. I change albums while my mother calls 911 and one of the neighbors comes in to keep her company. What I really want to do is prowl around Manhattan, buy a black leotard and tights, paint my eyes dark with kohl, and hook up with some kind of modern dance company. There's this dramatic bohemian woman named Martha Graham who talks about "the divine indiscipline" of the dance, and I would like to be her disciple. Contract! Release! It's the body, not the Torah, that contains the real truth. I try out some Graham technique on my own wraithlike body, sharply exhaling as I hollow out my middle, inhaling and then exhaling into an arch as I release.

It takes me a few minutes to realize what is happening just outside my bedroom door. A whole team of medics has invaded the apartment, and they are moving fast into my father's bedroom with a kind of hospital bed on wheels. Now I'm swaying way off to the side and recovering balance just before I fall to Dylan's promise that the answer I seek is blowing in the wind. When the song ends, I realize these medics are actually taking my dad out of the house in a big hurry. The turntable needle makes a scarring scratch in the record as I hastily lift it off its groove. I rush out of my room and stand on the side, watching the scene in stunned disbelief. My father is strapped onto a stretcher, his head and shoulders propped up a little. Before he is out the door, he manages to point at me and croak, "Look at her, she's dancing. This is her doing, she is happy to see me go." Then he adds, or I think I hear, "She wants me to die." There is nothing within me that can robustly counter his charges.

From that utterance on, I would be labeled a would-be patricide. What had my parents done to deserve a daughter who danced to Dylan when her own father was writhing in pain? How had they gone so wrong as to end up with a self-centered, godless teenager who would stop at nothing — not even this — to get her own way?

As they carry my father out, I try to catch my mother's eye, thinking she might draw a line, however faint, in the sand and set some limits to these outsized accusations. I'm not sure if these accusations are actually being uttered or if they are taking up permanent residence in my head, but I am profoundly spooked by my assumption of censure. I need someone to talk things over with, to sort this through. This is my mother, who just a few years earlier had rocked me in her arms when I dissolved into tears at not having breasts, the mother who had gone out of her way to buy me clothes that flattered my small size and immature figure, the mother who had encouraged me to wear padded bras so I wouldn't have to suffer relentless teasing. This is the mother with whom I had lain side by side at the end of every Sabbath day when my father and brother were in *shul*, just she and I watching the day fade away while sharing our most intimate thoughts. This is the mommy who knew how to heal every wound.

On this afternoon, her face grows dark, she shakes her head and averts my needy gaze. Though her desertion of me in the father-daughter wars was both endemic and incremental, it was in this moment of looking away, of deliberate silence, that she fully endorsed his indictment. And it was from that moment on that she and I could never again communicate with mutual trust.

Raphie and I sit cross-legged, each of us on our own rock overlooking the sea, sensing more than seeing one another in the descending night fog, listening now to our long exhalations against a soundtrack of crashing waves. After a particularly long exhalation, I start speaking again. He doesn't know all that transpired, but he knows enough to understand how this early drama has left its scars on my psyche. He also knows that in my own clumsy way I am now trying to make amends, to find ways to repair the rupture of the past. He is sensitive enough to understand that this effort implicates him as my first-born of the next generation, he intuits that there is in my seeking a nascent question of continuity.

Raphael tells me that he knows about all this, but he says it kindly, with openness, not in an attempt to cut me off or shut me down.

Raphael is silent and I resort to the bellows breath — rapid, shallow exhalations that sharply contract the abdomen as breath shoots out the nose. In yoga, these expulsions of air are known as the "breath of fire." One of the many (too many) biblical expressions for the wrath of God, "nose rage" *(charon af)*, pops into my mind. Yahweh's behavior, as unflinchingly recorded in the Torah, creates a template for anger in all its varieties: eruptive, slow simmering, consuming, righteous, vindictive, measured, fuming, reactive, incendiary, long lasting, despairing, and wildly destructive. My father's vituperative rage was utterly congruous with his self-appointed ambassadorship for God. As above, so below — so they say, and I know it to be true.

After our sixty rapid expulsions of air, Raphael speaks gingerly, with cautious determination. He tells me that I am more like my father than I think. He waits a few seconds to gauge the effect of his disclosure. I'm startled, but I accord him a good listen. He says that I have *"les idées reçues,"* fixed ideas, much the way my father did. I assume that the only worthwhile pursuits in this world are scholarly or legal or medical, and I am fixated on the idea that my son should cultivate his gift of exceptional intellect and be an achiever in the way of Jewish sons who make their mothers proud. I am withholding from him the approval of his chosen path as a percussionist much the way my father withheld his blessing from me.

I am quiet, receptive, and he grows a tad braver still. Perhaps it even has something to do with my unresolved feelings about giving up my own professional aspirations in dance. He is not entirely wrong. I thank him for his courage and his honesty in sharing and ask that we just sit and absorb it all for a while.

I look out on the ocean. It is no longer heaving and spewing. It is rather a softly breathing repository of everything that we have been able to share. I imagine the vessel of our wrath released, a message in a bottle floating far away and, if it were possible, bringing us succor from undiscovered lands.

Sweet Savor

All week long, my father was a caged panther, cursed with an obsessive mind and fueled by agitation. He prowled through a world of imagined slights, broken communication, nightmare scenarios, and a helplessness so utter he could only hitch his inchoate anger to the defense of a wrathful God.

But he was a religious man, an observant Jew, which meant that every week before Sabbath, my father would stop to bathe and change into fresh clothes. He seemed to understand that the prohibition against lighting fires on the Seventh Day was also a prohibition against igniting the hot flames of anger. From Friday night, when my mother dressed the table in white, cleared away workaday clutter, lit the candles, and we welcomed the heavenly angels, peace, *shalom,* reigned in our little house. To this day, *"Shabbat Shalom"* is a greeting I particularly savor.

Every Saturday evening of my childhood, with the Sabbath's departure, my father would return from the synagogue when three stars were out, and we would raise the flaming *havdala* candle to separate the sacred from ordinary time. We would pass around the aromatic spice box, and each of us in turn would close our eyes and inhale its aroma of cinnamon and clove. In this way we integrated the sweet savor of the Sabbath as an olfactory memory of serenity to be retained, if only such were possible, throughout the week.

Abraham Joshua Heschel, the spiritual mentor of B'nai Jeshurun, wrote with great beauty of the possibility of Sabbath. Still, he had to acknowledge that there is a tragic moment when the Sabbath inevitably departs. This is the moment when soul and spirit are separated and bereft. (I know it well.) The kabbalist text known as the *Zohar* suggests an antidote to this split: It tells us to reach for aromatic herbs "as their fragrance will reunite soul and spirit and make us glad." Myrtle, clove, and frankincense are all recommended for that purpose.

Heschel writes that the Sabbath is a "cathedral in time . . . the Sabbath is a window on eternity." It is also a sweet savor. Back in the Beforetime, it was customary to greet the Sabbath by dancing while waving branches of a myrtle tree. Every Friday night, the mystical luminary Isaac Luria would take two bunches of myrtle branches, bless them, and inhale their fragrance deeply. Anything inhaled on the breath (*neshima*) is integrated with the soul (*neshama*) as the Hebrew language confirms that breath and soul are one.

I am thinking about the pungent smell of anger, how God's rage and my father's were one, and wondering what it is I hope to reap for myself by attending the synagogue week after week. Where am I daring to meet this anger — in the simulation of my father's house, or in the house of the Lord, or in some new territory whose parameters are yet to be defined? How can I close my eyes and chant and sway my way into a spiritual safe haven immune to the anger that above all else has always marked the spot? Could it be that it is only through revisiting this explosive terrain that I can, in some way that is peculiarly mine, return home?

There is something curious about God as described in the Torah and our liturgy. Ours is a God who is constantly calling out for sweet savor. I first notice this in a Sabbath song called *"Ein Kelohenu,"* which has repetitive verses asking about the distinguishing qualities of our God. The verses conclude with a singular identifying feature: This is the God before whom our ancestors offered a fragrant offering of incense.

God repeatedly insists upon the *"re'ach necho'ach,"* the fragrant aroma that must accompany sacrifice. The Blessed Be He cannot get a handle on his quickness to anger, and for this he beseeches humankind for fragrance. So it is not only I who have forfeited a blessing. God, too, is desperately in need of a new benediction, a validation arising on a fresh and fragrant breath, one that only his human creations can provide.

I begin experimenting with inhaling natural fragrance emanating from essential oils such as frankincense and myrrh, cinnamon and clove, all of which are mentioned in the Bible as soothing to God. I open my own constricted soul to the blended savor of sacred oils, and in the rise and fall of this perfumed breath, I, too, begin to feel a shift. Could it be to experience this shared, reciprocal breath that I keep coming back to a House of the Lord, one that during my time away has been suffused with new life on the Upper West Side?

Still, there remain many limitations along the path of rapprochement. I will breathe Yahweh's chosen fragrance, but I will not consecrate my body to His ways. In the synagogue, I see some women wearing *yarmulkes*, binding themselves in the leather *tfillin* straps, and enveloping their bodies in a *talis*, a fringed prayer shawl. To me, this is a peculiar form of cross-dressing, a risky, ill-advised incursion into a male domain. It is a blurring of distinctions, and I could never sidle up to it. These women surely find in this ritual garb a safety, a trust, an intimacy that I am unwilling to consider. Yahweh has not carved inclusion in the covenant into my flesh, and He holds no sway over the pulsations of my pelvis. Contract: Suck up all of Creation into my own swirling cauldron. Release: Send forth my life force to a cosmos that knows not of Your ways.

Coming into womanhood, I put as much distance as I possibly could between a legislating Yahweh and myself. While in my mid-twenties, I received an invitation to dance abroad, beginning with a guest stint at the Bat Dor dance company in Tel Aviv. I bought a ticket for a journey that I thought would last at most a couple of years, but it was a couple of decades before my self-exile was complete and I began to contemplate a direction home.

Journey

Part Two

Because You Were a Stranger

We met in Paris when I was just passing through.

E.T. and I were two impatient strangers waiting in the lobby of a Parisian apartment building for the same unreliable lift. When at the same moment we opted for the stairs, we nearly knocked each other down. My romance with E.T. came into being more than three decades ago, with that near-collision on the bottom landing.

E.T. apologized madly, first in French, then in English, then in French again. I let him chase me, both of us laughing and breathless, up three flights of stairs, both of us assuming we'd meet up at the top.

He caught up with me in the pale light of the third-floor landing, at the threshold to the apartment where, through different friends, converging from different parts of the world, we had both been invited to the same dinner party. He learned later that I had always believed in "instant recognition," that is, in bumping into a stranger in some unexpected place in the middle of my wanderings and knowing that "he would change my life forever." Later, I told him that this was the first all-out Instant Recognition Alert I had ever experienced.

Here was a refined, dashing sort of a man into whose tender gaze I tumbled with all tranquility, somehow knowing he would never let me down. Later, I came to know that he fenced like a nobleman (well, almost) and made the best chicken soup ever (yes, really the best).

Although I was leaving early the next morning to work with the Bat Dor modern dance company in Tel Aviv, in that encounter I glimpsed a life-shifting possibility that I found impossible to shake: In France, I could recreate myself into whoever I thought it best to be. There was breathable relief knowing there was an ardent suitor awaiting me in a place called Paris, where my father's tyranny did not reign and where, unlike in then-provincial Tel Aviv, there was a category for the woman I was.

I pause for a word of explanation. Much as I was exhilarated by the vibrant energy of Israel and willing to participate in the birth of their own brand of contemporary dance (way before that pioneer art showed the promise it more than fulfils today), I was aware of a mismatch between the country's social categories and the woman I was. In the late 1970s, the Israelis managed gender relations by labeling women as specific "types." These labels were indicative of both a woman's character and her social role. To be a marriageable woman you had to be chaste, not too fanciful, presentable but not destabilizing, not too competitive, and preferably well under 25. A woman who was not ready to marry young and bear children, remain in the background, do all the housework, defer to her in-laws, and make her husband proud was something of an outcast. (These norms prevailed in secular as well as religious circles.) She might be stigmatized as a freakish intellectual, a bohemian artist, or at worst, a party girl who might be great to have around for an evening but was too much of a threat to the social order to take seriously.

Every Israeli male was a strutting King David when it came to his sexual prerogatives. On the home front, propriety would reign, while he as macho conqueror of women was subject to no law when on the prowl. Once seduced, women lost much of their value on the matrimonial market. I, for one, could recognize a no-win game with skewed rules when I saw one.

Rochelle was an American friend from high school who was determined to marry and mother in Israel. To that end, she withheld the surrender of her virginity for the longest time from Moti, her religious Zionist fiancé, who was the proud scion of a Sephardi rabbinic lineage. Finally, Moti persuaded Rochelle that her prudish attitudes were vestiges of an old diaspora mindset. Here in Israel, said he, even religious people were much more relaxed about biological imperatives. They were, after all, closer to natural rhythms; for generations they had been farmers, shepherds, planters, redeemers of the land. She came to understand that her clinging to outmoded sexual morés did not behoove her or their future lives together in this new land.

Before long, they were sleeping in villages and rising early to the vineyards. He came into her garden where the pomegranates flower, and, intoxicated, she gave him her love. Little did Rochelle know that while the budding flowers gave off their scent and the voice of the turtledove rose in the land, she was signing away her dreams.

When Moti returned to the north to discuss wedding plans with his prominent rabbinic family, he confirmed the rumors that had reached his inquiring parents' ears. Always less than enthusiastic about an American fiancée, his parents let him know that Rochelle had proven herself an ineligible candidate to join their family. After all, any woman who would give in to him would surely give in to others. The wedding was called off, and a few months later, he was rushed to the canopy with a bride with a more reliable pedigree.

It was all we, Rochelle's close friends, could do to keep her from resigning from life. Those months in Israel were marked by our efforts to keep this young woman from self-destructive despair — and the cautionary tale didn't end there. A few months into his marriage, Moti showed up at Rochelle's door imploring her to be his mistress. He insisted that his acquiescence to parental pressure had nothing to do with his still-ardent feelings for her. At that point, Rochelle's girlfriends became a consciousness-raising group, keeping her from further folly.

I didn't need to witness such dramas twice to intuit the precariousness of my own situation. There was much that could be said about the accomplishments of the State of Israel, but concern for the vulnerability and self-realization of its women was surely not one of them.

In Paris, I could seek sophisticated refuge in a cultural high ground, with a Jewish man (however unlearned and unaffiliated, still he wore a silver *mezuzah* around his neck) who welcomed my brand of expect-the-unexpected domestic bliss. He was an ebullient yet soulful kind of man, over-solicitous of his ailing mother and fluent in four languages, a wise and experienced man with whom I might mother children and give life a whole new start.

E.T. asked me to marry him the next summer while we were vacationing on a small Greek island, where we had fixed a rendezvous on my way home from Tel Aviv. I accepted his proposal by leaping off a high rock into the Aegean Sea, in a grand gesture of triumph over the terror and inevitability of self-renewal.

When I realized that I was engaged to be married, I thought it only appropriate to call my parents. Back then, this minimally courteous gesture required collecting a pile of coins and waiting on line at the island's only post office to place an overseas call. I counted on my mom's answering the phone and relaying the news to my father who, having survived his first heart attack and recently retired from teaching, often spent the day counting black sheep on the living-room couch. As luck would have it, this time it was Dad who took the call. As soon as he heard my voice, he barked something hostile and slammed down the phone. I had forgotten how furious he would have to be that I was off in Europe in the company of some strange man, "traipsing around" like a free spirit, indifferent to any sort of religious norms.

Although E.T. was nearly 40 years old, ours was to be his first marriage, and he looked forward to hosting an early summer wedding with the fashionable crowd he had often entertained as a debonair bachelor. (I was greeted coldly if politely by his social set; they did not get my appeal or my pedigree and mostly regretted the impending unavailability of a formerly gracious *célibataire*.)

The *de rigueur* wedding put a big crimp in my Great Escape plan. A wedding meant that before my life with E.T. officially got underway, my own parents and possibly even some of my relatives had to be hosted here in Paris. I cringed at the prospect of an actual wedding, but I also knew I could not deny it to E.T. or his parents and friends.

I would do whatever it took to see it through. I wanted to escape to another world where personal history might be abolished. My marriage to E.T. was clearly the perfect solution. This man had won my heart, and between us there was already deep trust. He needed my energy and optimism to jumpstart his own. We were two unconventional adults who had met when each was looking for some sort of kindred spirit. There was strong commitment without judgment or excessive possession. Early on, I had waking visions of our first-born child.

What's more, E.T. was a Jew, albeit a secular one. Born in Germany one month after the destructive rampage known as *Kristallnacht*, he was, when only a few months old, spirited away to France to wait out six more years of war posing as a Christian. His Jewish identity could therefore never involve the indelible psychic imprint it leaves on those born and raised with the knowledge from the start. Still, E.T. was certifiably a Jew — but a dispassionate, unengaged and unlearned one — meaning both that I could comfortably flee with him, and my family, though put off by my choice, would not be mourning me as if I were dead, as they likely would have had I married outside the faith.

My mom must have made an unusual effort to talk my father out of his morose refusal to celebrate my match. It took letters of inquiry and confirmation from several European rabbis before he begrudgingly accepted the fact that E.T. was Jewish. Several rabbis vouched for the extremely respected position E.T.'s parents enjoyed among community-minded if non-religious European Jews. Then there were a welter of conditions that had to be met in order for my father to behave with minimal courtesy at the wedding. We had to submit to the supervision of an Orthodox rabbi from the French *Consistoire* to seal our vows. In France back then — and even now to a great extent — our choice was either the sanitized and soulless province of the Germanic *Liberale* movement or the still-ghettoized preserve of the *halacha*-bound, Orthodox *Consistoire*. E.T. was indifferent, my family was adamant, and I didn't have it in me to wage all-out war.

I was already ill-disposed towards the agitated, overweight rabbi, with his strong Yiddish inflection and gnawed-off nails, who presided in the 16th *arrondissement* where we lived. In an earlier attempt to sample the community, I had once set out on a warm autumn evening, snack in hand, to have a bite in his *sukkah* with my husband-to-be. I don't know how it came into my mind to go there; I noticed the fruit-strewn hut when out walking, and I thought that for once it would be me introducing E.T. to a quaint novelty in the posh and polished neighborhood where he lived. No sooner did we settle at the table of the makeshift booth, however, than one of the rabbi's emissaries asked me to get up and cede my seat to a man. After all, eating in the outdoor, makeshift *sukkah* was an obligation for a man, whereas for a woman it was somewhere between an option and a frivolity. I packed up our dinner, grabbed a perplexed E.T., and left vowing never to return.

But this was the same rabbi in whose synagogue we were to be married, the very man who would preside. In a prenuptial visit, I tried explaining to him that no self-respecting woman wanted a marriage ceremony where her husband symbolically acquires her as chattel. The verbatim ceremony for Jewish marriage is all about a man bringing a woman into his domain. Since this was so much the reality in my case, I, the uprooted expatriate, felt the keen need for equilibrium in the ceremony. Could we not both exchange rings and spoken vows at the same time? It was fine with me if E.T., the acquiring husband, went first and I went second. I was not seeking to dominate or sabotage, only to carve out some personal meaning. Even some traditional ceremonies in the U.S. were allowing for this alteration. This rotund, tobacco-reeking, nervous man was not in the least interested in my needs and would not consider any abrogation of the ceremonial paradigm.

So, under duress, we accepted the restrictions on food, the prohibition of the champagne we adored, the delimited choice of wine, and the presence of a bearded man to preside over the uncorking of the sanctioned bottles. At the end of the wedding breakfast, we barely had a quorum or *minyan* for the Grace after Meals and Seven Blessings, as out of hundred and fifty or so in attendance, only my father, brother, and uncle, E.T., his father, and a handful of male friends of E.T.'s parents actually qualified as Jewish and male.

During our last prenuptial interview, the rabbi had carefully handed me instructions for the obligatory visit to the *mikve*, ritual bath, which had to take place after a safe interval with my menstrual cycle and a few days before the wedding. I listened in feigned attention. The *mikve* attendant would hand me a certificate attesting to my visit; said certificate I would hand to the rabbi at the time of the signing of the marriage contract behind closed doors just minutes before the public ceremony under the canopy.

Even if this stiff-necked, dandruff-flaked rabbi would have his way concerning the food and the wine and the ritual drama of the marriage, skewing the celebration of our love with an ill-suited series of symbols, he would not be submitting me to the ritual purity ordeal — no thanks, not me. Never would I demote myself into the contaminated and inherently impure issue of a bloodstain, worthy only to be dunked over and over in what would surely feel like a futile effort to come clean.

Submission to patriarchal authority is only one side of the Jewish-woman story, however. The other side is cunning and trickery in order to bring about desired outcomes in times of need. Think of Rebecca disguising her favorite son, Jacob, with the skin of a sheep so that his blind father, Isaac, might mistake him for his hirsute older brother, Esau, and thus give Jacob the blessing reserved for the first-born. Think of Tamar at the crossroads, disguised as a cult prostitute so that she could conceive and perpetuate the messianic lineage through the seed of Judah, her unsuspecting father-in-law. Think of me refusing to embark on my marriage feeling cold and clipped, invalidated and helpless, in the face of unrelenting humiliations.

The ceremony is scheduled for Sunday at noon, to be followed by a wedding buffet. It is already 12:15 when I arrive deliberately late with my *maman* by my side in the hired limo. We are rushed — after all the assembled are in their seats and waiting — into the rabbi's office for the requisite paperwork. Predictably, he asks me for the *mikve* certificate. I gasp and cover my mouth: In all the rush and excitement I left it at home! What choice does he have but to believe me? What choice do I have but to solemnly swear I will drop it off with him the very next day? What choice does he have but to accept my word?

E.T.'s father elegantly escorts my mother down the aisle. E.T. helps his mother, who is partially paralyzed by a stroke, slowly make her way to the wedding canopy. I am told there is not a dry eye in the house. Then, in something of an anti-climax, I am escorted down the aisle by my father, who is feeling reasonably satisfied with the match and the arrangements. For the scores of French Christians and a smattering of co-religionists gathered in the gender-segregated chapel, ours is one of the most anthropologically curious, oddly moving ceremonies they have ever seen.

It is again the fall holiday of Sukkot, some fifteen months later. I am seated on the couch in our living room nursing our four-month-old firstborn, Raphael Jacob. Suddenly, the floor under my feet and the glass windows are shaken in a terrible explosion. Moments later we smell smoke and hear the screeching of sirens. E.T. races down the four flights of stairs and up again to announce the news: Just down the street, the liberal synagogue on the rue Copernic has been bombed. (Our concierge referred to it as "the Israelite church.") I look down at my infant son and wonder how in the life that lies before him I will keep him safe. In my need to escape the suffocating censure of New York Jewish Orthodoxy, I birthed him back in the Old World, never for a moment considering its inhospitable history towards Jews. The greater danger seemed to me the withering away of his mother's spirit were there to be anything less than an ocean between her and the Orthodox crusaders back home.

Four people, three of them passersby, are killed in the terrorist attack, scores of others are injured, windows are blown out, and cars are wrecked up and down the fashionable street just a few hundred yards from where we live. A thoughtless Prime Minister Raymond Barre decries the incident in a telling way. He bemoans that terrorists who are targeting Jews end up killing "innocent French people" instead. The remark sends shockwaves through the Jewish community, sadly protesting its relegation to the ranks of those who are not innocent.

My little Raphael Jacob is dark haired and big brown eyed. He is an alert, curious, heartwarmingly cheerful infant. He is a circumcised and classically Jewish-looking child. I don't want to listen to the news and don't consider joining the massive protest that follows the synagogue bombing. I tenderly lower my baby into his crib when he has had his fill of my milk and watch him drift into undisturbed sleep. I find myself wishing, somewhat ashamedly, that for once this overbearing Jewish Question would by some miracle just forever fade away.

For my first seven years in France, I freelanced regularly for the International Herald Tribune while mothering two little boys in E.T.'s former bachelor pad, a fourth-floor walk-up on the fashionable avenue Victor Hugo. Despite its caché, the enclave was to me a repressive bourgeois preserve where I soon learned that a woman needed to dress a certain way if she was not to be taken for either an American *au pair* or a high-class foreign import-for-hire.

After seven years, we left avenue Victor Hugo at my instigation for life in a big, yellow-painted, 18th-century house tucked into a vine-covered courtyard off a cobblestone street in a charmingly preserved village in the Western suburbs. There, at the edge of a great wood leading to Versailles, I set myself up as a small independent publisher, putting out a quarterly newspaper for the well-heeled expatriate families living in the Paris area. Advertisers' enthusiasm for the buoyant expatriate market ensured that my first independent French enterprise was surprisingly vital. Now that we were out of town, we would have ample room for my newspaper office plus, of course, our two young boys, Raphael and Jonathan, our cats, Fido and Dido, a dog named Duke, and a pet snake whom we named, at my suggestion, Nachash.

It occurred to me only after we made the move that we were the only Jewish family living in the *vieux village*. I was an unknown, a foreigner, a creative nonfiction character to be animated anew in every different setting. My family name would mean nothing to the people I met in this distant land; no one would know of my past or confront me with their dashed expectations. In many ways, my experiment in recreating myself was working well. I could not have anticipated that life as an expatriate would eventually leave me feeling like a mermaid washed up on a remote, rocky beach, unable to speak in any language of the depths in which I was fashioned.

During this period, I found myself mysteriously drawn to the Marais, an ancient if rapidly gentrifying Parisian quarter that has long been the center of the city's Ashkenazi Jewish life. I would often take the commuter train from my suburban home to its central street, the rue des Rosiers, whose sights and sounds were a cacophony of nostalgia and daily hustle. The heyday of its commercial and community life had been between the wars, before the roundups and murderous deportations of Jews carried out by the French police in World War II. The Marais was a neighborhood to which I would find myself returning again and again, even if its nostalgia rankled.

So drawn was I to the odor of Jewish rye and garlic pickles, the Hebrew notices tacked up on every wall, the sound of a beggar woman belting out Yiddish songs from her seat on the sidewalk, the black hats in a hurry brushing by skulking gay guys, that I began doing a freelance reportage on the various layers of life here. Then one day, on a whim, I decided to share an inexpensive Marais office with a friend on a part-time basis. Thus I legitimized my return to this neighborhood again and again. Its crowded streets positioned me right on the edge of my comfort zone. Its kosher snack bars displayed the words to obligatory prayers writ large, like archaic wallpaper. Esoteric titles in English, French, Hebrew, Yiddish, and Arabic lined the windows of its many Jewish bookstores, attracting me as much as they repelled me.

The streets were narrow and winding, and I was constantly twisting my heels on its uneven cobblestones. I remarked how the 16th-century buildings were huddled together, leaning on each other, as if to hold each other up by communal faith. On the days before Yom Kippur, I glimpsed caged chickens squawking in an alleyway in anticipation of an ancient ceremony of absolution in which a sacrificial fowl will be whirled senseless over the head of some fervent penitent before its kosher slaughter.

This was the sort of environment I had planned to scrupulously avoid, yet somehow I couldn't get enough of it. These were streets crammed with blatant messages and unspoken secrets. Once, a car protruding from a driveway on the narrow rue des Rosiers conspired with a stalled van to block my path. There was no room for me to squeeze by, and no escaping the bright red decal pasted on the back of the van: *And you shall love the Lord thy God with all your heart and all your soul and all your might,* the decal screamed in red Hebrew letters. I would have given anything to get away from these strident reminders, yet nothing could keep me from returning to this quarter again and again.

On one unassuming side street, there was a humble synagogue housed inside a storefront. Through the glass window I could see bearded men poring over a parchment scroll, laid out on a table lined with rows of burning memorial candles. By then, I was careless about lighting such a candle for my father, who died when Raphael was 4 and Jonathan was just a few months old. I had no clear feeling about whether or not I would remember to do so this year, but I stood there peering in, with uncertainty tensed up beneath my ribs.

Of all things Jewish that I was determined to leave behind, it was the loss of the Sabbath that haunted me the most. There was a mysterious malaise that would often lay me low on Saturdays, and only on Saturdays, for the many years I lived in France. Even if I managed to keep everyone close to hearth and home for Friday-night dinner, in the absence of community or firm conviction, Saturdays were relegated to ordinary chore-filled days devoted to supermarkets and hardware stores, home repair, restaurant lunches, and shopping in town.

I would awaken on the Seventh Day with visceral dread and a terrible feeling of incongruity with myself and with the life I was leading. My profound unease was followed by the onset of a migraine, this indisposition accompanied by an incapacitating fit of depression that would loosen its grip on me only at sunset. My grief was abysmal but without specificity. It took me a long time to acknowledge how deep and unnamed were my lost-Sabbath blues. Whenever I intuited the source of my anguish, I harshly told myself that my *Sehnsucht,* soul-sickness, was only a vestige of a former state of consciousness. I would remind myself, not always kindly, that I was no longer a believer, no longer a member of that club. What's more, I had come to this side of the pond specifically to cut ties. There was no place in my chosen life for vestigial nostalgia.

The get-a-grip approach did nothing to improve my weekly head-aches, and the resulting inner conflict only darkened my despondent moods, which often triggered outbursts of ill temper that seemed to well up from a deep source. Now and then my thoughts would wander to Hesh and his stories of the Acher. I knew very well how a single person could yearn and spurn, care deeply and not want to know that she does. More than one nonbeliever has argued with ancient voices all through the night.

I would often recall a Sabbath story that my mother used to tell me, about how every man is accompanied home from the synagogue on Friday night by a good and a bad angel, walking beside him on either side. If, upon entering his foyer, they find that the laws have been neglected and the Sabbath dishonored by rancor or sin, it is the evil angel who invokes the Almighty: "May the next Sabbath be as this one." And as the evil angel wishes it, so it comes to pass. But if the Sabbath is in good order, if all forbidden things have been set aside and a peaceful atmosphere reigns, it is the good angel who blesses the house: "May the next Sabbath be as this one." And as he utters it, so it comes to pass.

I wanted my two young sons, Raphael and Jonathan, to know a little something of the Sabbath spirit — but why bother with the Sabbath in the midst of a self-consciously secular lifestyle? I could not fully explain my attachment, even to myself. It was like an old, beloved song that needed to be sung, even if only in a whisper, just for a few minutes, and slightly off key. It was a longing for a moment of stillness, when all the realms of Creation, from the highest to the lowest, were united. Perhaps it had something to do with a vaguely felt need for union within myself. Whatever it was, I longed to share something of the Sabbath's peace and harmony with my children.

I would do what I could to simulate a Friday-night *shabbat* meal. Sometimes I went so far as to see to it that the silver was polished and the white embroidered tablecloth spotlessly clean. The challah loaves I had purchased the day before on the rue des Rosiers were unwrapped and covered again with a satin embroidered cloth. I would insist, as the family gathered around the specially dressed table, that all the televisions, computers and stereo systems be silenced. It was hard for them to understand, as I did, that this was the only way to usher in even a little of the Sabbath's otherworldly glow.

E.T. and the children would watch in respectful silence as I covered my head with a lace scarf and lit the candles, then circled the flames three times and covered my eyes to recite the weekly blessing. Some Friday evenings, I stood for a few extra moments, murmuring my own prayer to whatever forces were at work, asking for reconciliation, a meeting point of the opposites that, even in the numbing glow of the Sabbath lights, kept on struggling within.

E.T. had never learned to read Hebrew, but to please me he willingly recited the *kiddush* prayer in transliteration, holding the silver cup high. When he finished reciting, I always prompted the boys to answer "amen."

One Friday night, Pablo, the devilishly handsome 12-year-old son of a French mom and Trinidadian father, both non-Jewish, was with us in Paris, his first time at a *shabbat* table. Jonathan, our youngest son, had knocked over some juice on the white embroidered tablecloth, and when E.T. began to make a fuss, I reminded him that on this, the Sabbath eve, there was no room for rancor or ire. Apparently, my words had the desired effect, and we all settled into a renewed serenity.

Twenty-two years later, Pablo, now married with children of his own, wrote to say that he had never forgotten what he glimpsed that night at our Sabbath table. "I came from a troubled and unsettled world. The idea that a tradition could unite people in such a feeling of peace deeply impressed me. I marveled at a religion that could defuse chaos and soothe anger, even if just for an evening. My fascination with Judaism dates from that dinner." Imagine our surprise to read that after years of study and serious thought, he was completing the steps for his conversion to Judaism. Pablo had been observing the laws of *kashrut* as well as the Sabbath for years, even abstaining from coming to work on Friday night in the nightclub he managed.

On the Sabbath eve, two angels, one on each side, accompany us in our coming and goings. That night there was one angel who lingered, a curious, optimistic, iconoclastic sort of angel whose wings folded tenderly into the groove of my failings. Those wings silently brushed us with fate in a moment of grace. That moment gave wings to unimagined Sabbaths that have come to pass, as well as endless others that are still waiting to be born.

The 1980s and '90s, when I married, mothered, worked, and made friends in France, can be characterized as one of the honeymoon periods in the long and often-hostile relationship of France with its resident and immigrant Jews. This is not to say that being Jewish in France was ever a non-issue. How could it be? In the streets of the Marais, everywhere, there are plaques commemorating the deportation of school children right out of their classrooms, more plaques commemorating families who were awakened and hauled away in the early dawn to their eventual deaths. One Eastern European bakery on the rue des Rosiers, where I went religiously for a hot cheese *borek* (and sometimes a vial of iced vodka to go with it), still had posters of disappeared children, whose presumed deaths were never documented, asking if any of these missing persons might still be identified.

In 1980, Raymond Barr's thoughtless remarks in the wake of the rue Copernic synagogue bombing poured salt on an uncauterized wound. It was not until 1995 that Jacques Chirac officially apologized for the previously denied role the French actively played in the mass murder of its own Jewish citizens during the Second World War. As a result, most French Ashkenazi Jews kept a low profile, deeming discretion to be the better part of valor. The cautious survivors of the death camps cringed at the exuberance of the Sephardi Jews, whose influx in the early '60s from the former colonies of North Africa injected the moribund community with unbridled pride.

There were other attitudes that caused me personal consternation as a transplanted New York Jew lightly tiptoeing through a predominantly gentile milieu in the crusty and conservative Old World. One day, during the holiday of Passover, a self-effacing woman who worked as an assistant to E.T. in his home office invited our two boys to her house for lunch. I agreed, asking only that she not serve them bread or pasta in token observance of the holiday's dietary laws. She grew bold as she sat me down for what felt to me like a long-awaited chat. Why did I insist that my children be different from the others? Didn't I realize what a burden that was? It was surely a social disadvantage that brought with it no compensatory reward. Besides, it rubbed people the wrong way. If I insisted on living this way, it must be because I thought it better, but if my way was better, then the implication, to which French people would certainly take exception, is that their way was not as good.

Try as I might — and this was neither the first nor the last time I engaged in this effort — I could not convince her, or other French folks, that individuals could honor their own traditions without implying that others were somehow inferior for living differently. The dignity of difference, so intrinsic to American multiculturalism, could not strike a resonant chord in a country where the social leveling via *liberté, égalité, fraternité* neutralized all particularities of contributing cultures.

The irony was that I considered my own observance of Judaism to be token, a bare-bones nod to a past from which I could not entirely sever myself. We belonged to no congregation, we did not observe Jewish holidays in any fullness, our Sabbath lasted for around half an hour before it was interrupted and we returned to the concerns of ordinary life. My children had little formal Jewish education, most of our friends were not Jewish, our home was not kosher. We had visited Israel only once, and this was because my mother made a gift to us of the trip. Yet even the most minimal signs of allegiance to a sub-group was cause for serious consternation among many of the French people we knew.

After we returned to New York City in 2001, people we met at B'nai Jeshurun often asked E.T. and me if we left France because of a rise in anti-Semitism. The thought may have crossed our minds, but it held no sway. We saw our move as motivated by other, more personal concerns.

Raphael had been living in my Upper West Side apartment throughout his undergraduate studies at NYU; the time had come for me to make the rent-stabilized apartment my primary residence, if I was to avoid the real and present danger of losing it. My mother, who was by then in her eighties, had been diagnosed with multiple myeloma, a form of blood cancer, and I wanted to be nearby to care for her. Jonathan was a high school senior, about to enter McGill University in Montreal. I had transferred ownership of my small Paris communication company, and there was nothing left anchoring me there. I had fulfilled my contract with France and was ready to turn the page. I was suffering from a hard-core case of *Sehnsucht* and needed to return to my native land. Anti-Semitism was simply not a factor in my conscious decision-making.

There was something intriguing in the way well-meaning BJ folks would broach the subject. After all, they were not commiserating with refugees from Eastern Europe or escapees from some backward Moslem dictatorship. They were addressing people who had left one of civilization's brightest stars, *la belle France*, an acknowledged bastion of culture and enlightenment, and a democracy that, unlike theirs, had somehow managed to balance social welfare with regulated capitalism while extending quality education and health care to all. The idea that even in such a place, cosmopolitan citizens such as E.T. and I might have had to flee because of a resurgence of religious hatred sent a frisson of horror up people's spines. I was almost sorry to have to disappoint their sincere if premature expressions of sympathy. We could not offer up that admission for the simple reason that, in our conscious experience, it hadn't been true.

Yet after our big move, as the reports of anti-Jewish violence in France reached alarming peaks in 2002 into 2003, and as the well-meaning questions proliferated, I found myself examining memories I heretofore had preferred to whitewash or forget.

I had experienced both extremes in what truly was a story of love and hate in my adopted land. In Marly Le Roi, the cobblestone village at the edge of the forest where we were the only Jews, I had met good people who revered me more than any compatriots ever would for my pedigree and my knowledge. One friend's mother was a renowned Bible scholar, a French woman named Germaine Colas, who encouraged all devoted Catholics to learn Hebrew so they could get closer to the original meaning of God's words. She argued against reading about Jesus' religious life and heritage in a French translation that came from the Latin that came from the Greek; better to read it at the source.

Through Germaine, word got around that an American Jewish woman who was from a rabbinical lineage and educated in biblical Hebrew lived with her family in the village. We were treated with what I can only call reverential respect by this small coterie of seekers. From time to time, Germaine or her students would call to consult me about a word or a phrase. Our conversations were nuanced, passionate, and wholehearted. Germaine once told me that her husband was convinced I had a direct pipeline to God.

After seven years, we moved from Marly to another house in the next town, across from the International Lycée, where both my boys went to school. I went out for my first morning coffee in a nearby café. By 11:00 or so in the morning, it was not unusual for French workers to enjoy their first *pastis* of the day. There was a red-eyed man a few feet from me at the counter who looked to be well past his first drink. It took a few minutes for me to absorb the gist of his slurred monologue. He was saying that he was only sorry that Hitler hadn't "finished the job." The fact that Jews were still around was the only thing for which he could "fault the Führer." Nobody within earshot uttered a word of protest. For me, it was an intensely uncomfortable moment of truth.

Hadn't I made this enormous detour in my life just so I would lose my nagging preoccupation with the Jewish Question? Hadn't I chosen expatriation just so I could distance myself from Judaism as the central core of my identity? Hadn't I given up so much that fueled my passion for life in New York just so I could gain a certain freedom from religious constraints? There was nothing compelling me to reveal myself to this man. No one would know, or even blame me, if I simply let a drunken lout get away with his mutterings.

I put down my empty coffee cup, lit a cigarette, and walked up to the man. I told him that I found it curious and, for that matter, most disagreeable that even though we had never met, he seemed to have a lot of opinions about my family and me. He looked stunned and confused. I told him I was alarmed to hear that he'd like to see us all come to great harm. Pretending not to understand a word I said, he found his unbalanced way out of the café. The others averted their gazes; no one joined or opposed me. I was living in a world without echoes.

My longing to return to New York was alive from the first day I moved to Paris. As the biblical Chochma (Wisdom) says of herself, it was "set-up from everlasting, there from the beginning." Choosing to put an ocean's divide between my new family and the religious tyranny of my old one never implied disconnection from all that gave my life its fascinating rhythm in New York. I had moved, married, and become a mom assuming that France would be an ideal starter kit for our family. Once E.T.'s parents died (which they both did within four years of our marriage), once I could stand up for myself with my own family, I was certain we would leave behind the dampened spirits and low gray skies of the Old World for the crisp light and promise of adventure that to me was New York, *toujours* New York.

On my many trips back to New York over the years, I was accustomed to the envy my lifestyle induced in the startling number of people who harbored naïve dreams of living in Paris. To them I would willingly concede that the food was exceptional, the architecture pleasing, the mood poetic. The flowers were dazzling in spring, conversations sparkled with cultural sophistication, working moms had institutionalized child-care, and there was something magical in the light of summer days that lasted until 11:00 at night. I was never so ungrateful as to complain about my domestic or professional life. I took socialized medicine for granted. My live-in *au pairs*, the privileges accorded journalists, the diversity of our social life, the solidity of my marriage, my freedom to travel were all enviable, to be sure.

I was not able to convey the sense of disconnection that haunted me wherever I went, the non-belonging expressed in a constant, low-grade yearning for a return to something that for the longest time I could not name. Sometimes I would find myself half praying: *Oh Lord, teach me how not to yearn, even if yearning — for completion, or Zion, or redemption with its promise of absolution of yearning — is all I've ever known.*

There is no denying the gifts of French civilization. The level of literacy, cultural sophistication, and art appreciation at the average dinner party eclipses that at any of America's top universities. The young men have good manners, the young women have style, every boutique window is a design gem, and the simplest people know the importance of slowing down, closing shop, and gathering around the hearth to share a memorable meal. The French cherish socializing and preparing food as values in themselves; work is something to be tolerated out of necessity, but could never, as it does in the States, come to dominate or define a whole life. There is an emphasis on clear thinking, the construction of a classical argument, along with a reverence for language. Sensuality — how things smell, feel, look, and taste — graces ordinary life in ways for which we Americans understandably hunger.

For all those appreciable perks, there was a vast human territory wherein I could find little satisfaction. For lack of a better term, let me call it the psycho-emotional plane: France is the biggest consumer of anti-depression and anti-anxiety medication in Europe. When it comes to the more complex affairs of the heart, they would rather anesthetize than feel. The reigning Lacanian school of psychoanalysis scoffs at the notion of helping people feel better. The goal is theoretical understanding of the impossibility of happiness, given our inherent condition. This intransigent pessimism suffuses a land where actual progress in self-seeing, emotional honesty, and relational skills are not revered, where despite the emphasis on courtesy, a cynicism regarding human limitations is the common excuse for a moratorium on personal growth. Unhappy people, famished for a core sense of who they are, grow old sadly repeating hollow slogans, mumbling that it's all the fault of somebody else.

Americans are caught off guard when I tell them that during my sojourn in France it was difficult to admit my devotion to Insight Meditation without raising suspicions of belonging to a cult. Even my enthusiasm for yoga with a little mood-setting chanting alarmed some people for its presumed affinity to brainwashing. This extreme mistrust of anything remotely religious or doctrinaire stems from the bitter struggle of the secular Republicans with the stranglehold of the Catholic Church over state policy and people's minds. The legacy of the secular rationalists' victory is a reflexive disdain for anything even vaguely suggestive of a spiritual quest. Spirituality, according to the refined French intellect, implies sloppy thinking and susceptibility to hocus-pocus, while the shared creed of Republicanism is founded on clear-minded logic as to what constitutes a fair, just, and generally benevolent society.

There is, in France, a virulent crusade (and I choose that last word deliberately) against religious influence in the life of the State. Those who would banish all vestiges of a Catholic-affiliated past are as inflexible as are those who in other countries try to impose religious law. In France, headscarves, crucifixes, and skullcaps are banned from public buildings. (It does not seem to bother anyone that all Catholic holidays are "official" and that for every day on the secular calendar, there is a corresponding saint for whom the day is named.)

Religious sentiments and attitudes cannot, however, be legislated out of existence, even if campaigns against exterior signs can triumph. The more the influence of Catholicism is repressed, the more it retreats underground. Unexamined, these religious attitudes seep into sectors of French life, where they wreak systemic damage.

Centuries of Augustinian self-loathing have never been confronted, nor have they been effectively deconstructed out of the land. Instead, like some radioactive waste, Catholic self-loathing has seeped into the soil, where it poisons all that takes root. For starters, the disavowed Catholic doctrine of Original Sin follows the path of least resistance and becomes the reigning ethos of France's elementary schools. Within those repressive walls, every child is guilty until proven innocent, every 6-year-old is worthless until proven redeemed. French people rarely escape nationalized education without some serious self-esteem issues. I spent much of my time counterbalancing that pernicious influence in my own boys' lives, and trying to point out its biases to whoever would accord me a listen.

Mlle Catherine M. was anything but happy to see me walk into her life. For all her pretense of deconstructing identity, her ego was maniacally dedicated to self-preservation. Catherine was (and still is) the editor-in-chief of *Art Press*, a post-modern art magazine she founded in the late 1960s to speak in deconstructivist language about contemporary arts and letters. At the time she and I met, I was no longer publishing my own paper but doing consulting work for other clients. I was hired by her publisher to launch a bilingual, international edition of *Art Press*. It soon became clear that Catherine harbored a real terror of releasing her magazine into the world beyond her slavishly devoted clique. Her command of English was shaky at best, and her fears of exposure were well-founded: the convoluted vapidity of the original text was mercilessly revealed when subjected to translation, and it became a real case of the Emperor's New Clothes when the self-referential jargon was limited to the literal translation that a controlling Catherine insisted upon. For a while I had to convey her fiats to my translators, but after an issue or two, we relaxed them. Catherine protested every step of the way. Let's just say that she and I never became the best of friends.

I began with no awareness of the gaps that yawned between my own sensibilities and those of the trendy deconstructivists. I had never met people who taught that the only thing that meant anything was language and refused to grant meaning to the things whose complexities most of us ordinary mortals spend our lives navigating: relationships, connection, a path through parenting, the soulful resonance of beauty, pleasure, personal identity, and most inimical of all to these thinkers, the carving out of some spiritual dimension to human experience.

I had never met self-styled intellectuals who supported one another in, to me, an incomprehensible campaign against meta-meaning. While some of us stunted types were still struggling with all that old-fashioned stuff, the post-modern elite were busy deconstructing it and letting one another know in coded language how it felt to live in the sterile landscape of all that lies beyond such pedestrian concerns.

Looking back, I wonder if I should have taken on the assignment in the first place. On the pro-side, the gentlemanly *Art Press* publisher was charming and the pay was good. I had all-expenses-paid trips to New York several times a year, and a team of translators who needed the work. For all these reasons, even as I learned more about the post-modernists, I walked into hostile territory with my eyes wide open.

Still, the warning signs could not have been clearer. In a recent cover story, *Art Press* had singled out C.G. Jung and Mircea Eliade for special "demonization." Their alleged crime was unfettered "obscurantism." In targeting these two thought leaders, *Art Press* had picked on the two most influential thinkers in my own young life. When, at the age of 17, I had to face the unavoidable evidence that I was no longer a believer in God's revelation of Absolute Truth through his Torah as given on Sinai and interpreted through the rabbinic tradition, I found myself floundering in a terrifying void. The choice between adherence to a codified world and a complete absence of meaning created too great a gap. My discovery of Carl Jung and Mircea Eliade, with their understanding of archetypal patterns and mythic consciousness, threw me a lifeline. I can't elaborate here on the many ways in which Jung and Eliade saved my life as a renegade seeker. Suffice it to say that Catherine M. and I had singled out the same two guys, only for wholly opposite reasons.

The post-modernist *Art Press* crowd vilified Jung and Eliade because they propagated "the repressed religious element in secular societies." This was "an element" against which *Art Press* was a self-appointed vigilante, as expressed in its own mission statement. Here again, I found myself in the odd position of resenting those who campaigned against "the repressed religious element" as much as I had disagreed with those back home who insisted that we live by it. Their vigilantism against leftover religious influence expressed itself in a ruthless denial of meta-meaning in adult life, a campaign that had some sensational results.

Catherine M. caused a furor in 2001 with the publication of her book, *The Sexual Life of Catherine M.*, in which she wrote with graphic, laconic detail and an anesthetized air about orgies during which she could have sex with twenty to thirty anonymous partners a night. She was, by fiat, the only woman allowed within the confines of these gatherings. (This went a fair distance towards explaining her hostile reception of me in the magazine office, where she also reigned solo and supreme.) In her book, she managed to freeze-dry eroticism into a barren and sterile wasteland. Catherine's triumph was using language to bring us sex meticulously described as detached sensation and nothing more. It was her right to do so, even if for me and many homo sapiens I know, sex has long been about absolutely everything. Those of us lagging behind needn't have been troubled. There was Catherine M. to the rescue on the late-night talk shows, letting everyone know that we could lie back on the hood of a car, open our orifices to random strangers, bang our way past all this psychic baggage, and finally live free.

So by the time Catherine M. (herself not a bad example of the lapsed and luxuriantly self-loathing Catholic) had to accept the translation of *Art Press* into a language she could not censor, her book had catapulted her to fame. As her giggly voice floated from the nightly television talk shows, I packed twenty-two years of my family's life into ever-growing piles of cardboard boxes, sorted, taped, and labeled for transport. I left Catherine M. and the other French intellectuals to their fiercely defended turf, which I declare to have been as conducive to human evolution, not to mention connection, as the landscape of the moon.

Purim Play

I need to plot my long-awaited return from exile to my native city, but suddenly there is alarming news: I am being sued for eviction by my New York landlord who has finally looked with a covetous eye on my spacious, rent-stabilized, eighth-floor perch.

The apartment has been my fallback position in the universe ever since I was a Columbia University graduate student. I've unfailingly covered the reasonable rent, returning for visits several times a year, keeping my homestead safe for what every year I convinced myself was my imminent return. During the passing decades, my Upper West Side block has been transformed from a shady side street known for its dangerous halfway house to a charming, brownstone-lined lane in a riverside neighborhood now ranking among the most desirable in Manhattan. Even though my place was but one of thousands of apartments in his portfolio, I had to expect that the Big Bad Landlord would sooner or later counter my legal right to the lease.

Now in his first year at NYU, Raphael is occupying the apartment with a roommate. My French-born-and-raised son is coming of age within the very same walls that once absorbed the secrets of my own youthful excesses. I am aware that he and I are haunted by the same demons. I know the dangers of his let's-keep-pushing-the-envelope curiosity, but I also know I have to leave him to his own process without the interference that stands in the worst tradition of overbearing Jewish moms.

I return from New York City to our new home in the Parisian suburb, the one across the street from the prestigious International Lycée, and mourn my separation from my native town and oldest son. My homesickness for New York rages like a fever. Reason dictates that I must now await Jonathan's *lycée* graduation and eventual enrollment in a North American college before making my definitive move back home. I am undone by the news: The building has long ago gone co-op under a non-eviction plan. My Manhattan landlord, intent on wresting the apartment away from me and putting it up for sale, is now suing me for non-primary residency in mid-lease. Never before have I felt so vulnerable. I cannot possibly afford the more than one million dollars the apartment is worth on the market, and I benefit from no insider's price. Stunned that Raphael's occupancy does not protect my rights, I fly "home" to seek legal counsel and prepare what I hope will be a persuasive defense.

Throughout the flight from Paris and the taxi ride from the airport, I dread what awaits me. As soon as I open the door, I am greeted by a giant, unruly mass of registered letters, their bold oversized type terrifying in their threatened finality. I have some thirty days to reply before the sheriff gets here and throws my son and me and any other occupants and all our belongings onto the street. I am reminded that this is not the anything goes, decaying New York I left behind in the late '70s; this town is now a coveted hot spot of savvy real estate magnates, and for me to have a shot at regaining a foothold, I'd better get my wayward ducks in a pretty persuasive row.

After a sleepless night, at 8:59 a.m., the phone rings. It's the tenant lawyer, responding to my many urgent messages, and she urges me to come to her office without delay.

The tenant lawyer is a tiny, spunky Italian woman with plenty of experience in this war-torn domain. She informs me that we have no choice but to head for a deposition — a legal term for a kind of inquisition in which the attorneys are entitled to investigate every corner and crumb of what up until now has been my utterly unofficial life. In a closed room, during a day-long interrogation, I will be required to lay on the table papers documenting the details of my daily whereabouts for the past three years. I will also be subjected to questions about my marriage, my mothering, my professional activities, my wanderings, and my allegiances, none of which conforms to any conventional patterns. The landlord will then assess if he has enough damning evidence to move to trial, and a court judge will then rule on the crucial question of whether or not I can claim my apartment as a primary residence in which, according to the rules of rent stabilization, I am still entitled to live.

I leave the lawyer's City Hall office so deflated I can hardly breathe. This much-longed-for city is crushing me with its cruelly surging economic might. I have been rejected before, exiled by a wrathful father, banished by my own refusal to conform to the law. But is it possible that through the legal maneuvering of a savvy landlord, the entire city and its implacable laws can now conspire to expel me definitively from its midst?

I wander through the lunchtime crowds with barely the voice to ask a street vendor for a bottle of water. For the first time, I know what it feels like to be part of the human refuse that this city's pitiless wheels grind over every day. I continue uptown, feeling faint, and with a problem tooth vaguely starting to throb. Other than a glass of grapefruit juice and several black espressos, I haven't fed my knotted stomach anything since my arrival from Paris the day before. I keep walking, past the art galleries and boutiques of Soho, marveling at how so many high-functioning people have mastered their insouciant lives, and bemoaning the intractable mess I have made of my own.

Collapsing on a bench in Washington Square Park, I note for the first time what a fine day this truly is. After a long winter, the sun is warming, the breeze is fresh, there is not a cloud in the vaulting New York sky. Here in front of my glazed eyes is a lanky, Mediterranean-looking kid kicking a soccer ball around in the dry dust. I refocus: It's my very own lanky, Mediterranean-looking kid, a singular hybrid of French swain and New York waif, kicking the ball with carefree coordination on this unofficial green of the NYU campus, and he's unaware that his mother is sitting just a few yards away lamenting their terrible plight.

Now Raphael flashes me a smile and saunters over to the bench. I am about to share something of the day's woes when a proselytizing Orthodox Jew heads straight toward us. I hastily instruct Raphael to tell him we are not Jewish so he won't pester us today. The Hasid approaches me first.

"I'm not Jewish," I blurt out, turning away.

"I am Jewish," Raphael replies. "But," he continues most civilly, "if you don't mind, I don't want to put on *tfillin* today."

The man finds no argument with Raphael's easy candor. He has only come to tell us that today is a happy Jewish holiday. It is Purim, the commemoration of the long-ago day when the Jews of Shushan defeated the Persian armies sent to destroy them. This is a day for laughter and carousing, for masquerading and gift-giving, for listening to the recitation of the ancient *megilla* scroll. Raphael thanks the man, who goes on his way.

This is a surprise and yet it isn't. On the very day the Jews of the world are celebrating their triumph over legendary enemies, I am feeling crushed to the bone. My landlord enemy and all his legal advisors — Kaplan, Goldman and Rosenblum, Esquires, Inc. — are all Orthodox Jews. These are my accusers, who are obliging me to seek exoneration for my self-styled (and hence transgressive) lifestyle. It is these men who would have me dragged from my foyer and stoned at the city gates. And it is before the eyes of these men that I am called upon, if not to atone, then to justify and redeem myself. For those who esteem the letter of the law, I am, of course, an outlaw to be condemned into exile anew. Those willing to allow for the spirit of the law may agree with me that none of my adversaries will suffer a significant loss if I am allowed, despite my obvious sins, to hold onto a small, rented corner of their vast empires.

"Why won't you even speak to him?" Raphael wants to know. I turn away, unwilling to give him the favor of a reply.

Raphael just doesn't seem to grasp the real danger we are in if we continue to violate the laws governing our rights to tenancy. I learn that his new friend, Jean Dominique, a homeless black saxophonist from French Guyana, has been living at our house for the past two months. My new friend the lawyer, whose advice costs me hundreds of dollars per hour, strongly advises me to get rid of anyone who might be considered an outright illegal occupant at this more-than-delicate time. When I announce this to Raphie, I am dangerously vulnerable to his wrath.

With barely concealed fury, he lets me know there is no reason someone who is cold and hungry and righteous should have to freeze in the streets so that someone as rich and greedy as the landlord can simply continue to get richer. He doesn't see how it hurts these avaricious creeps if his friend continues to find shelter under our roof. I keep telling him that my absence in France has technically violated the terms of the lease, and now we have to face the scrutiny of the law. I have a very expensive lawyer whose advice I feel compelled to follow.

Later that evening, we are sitting in the kitchen. Raphael picks up a wooden spatula and whacks the kettle hard.

"If we've violated any kind of law, it should be stricken from the books." *Wham.* An overhanging pot swings menacingly from his blow. "There is such a thing as a higher law, you know, way higher than whatever it is a money-grubbing landlord stands for in a housing court." *Crash,* he smacks two pot covers together.

He punctuates his remarks with a few more sharp blows to the kettle. I grab the spatula out of his hand. He replaces it with a metal whisk.

"Look, Raphael, I have no fallback position. I can't possibly afford another place in New York. I lose this place and I'm out, and so, incidentally, are you."

"By making Jean Do leave, you are acquiescing to those who are ruining the planet with avarice and greed."

I feel like grabbing the whisk and smashing it across his face. Instead I roughly yank the window open to get some air. The frame is as rickety as I feel.

"Okay, Mom, take it easy, why are you crying?"

He lays down the whisk next to the spatula. There are no more slaps or beats, smashes or shuffles.

"But, Mom, you always said it's in the difficult times that we are called upon . . ."

"Raphie, stop it. I ignored your friend being here for as long as I could. I just can't anymore."

"It's all right, Mom, he's leaving, he knows he has to. What more do you want?"

I turn around and face him. "I want you to understand me."

It is nearly 11:00 at night, and Raphie will be going out now to meet up with Jean Do and check out the clubs. Before leaving, he comes over to see me in the kitchen, where I am seeking solace in a hot cup of herbal tea. Usually after such outbursts, it takes several hours for each of us to simmer down enough to be able to tolerate one another's presence. But a contrite Raph re-enters my atmosphere with a certain temerity. It seems he has something important to say.

He tells me he has a good idea for me, something that will make me feel better, something to soothe my nerves. He suggests that come Friday night, I go diagonally across the street and join the service at this synagogue called BJ. Now I am truly astonished. He is anything but a synagogue-goer, and his recent explorations with Jean Do have been more inspired by the New Testament than the Old. Still, he has reason to believe this will be a good move for me at this time. Then he swings one huge conga in its carrying bag over his shoulders. He assures me he's gotten used to bearing that weight on his back. For a second he puts his burden down and comes to give me a quick kiss before setting out into the night.

My eyes are closed, and a weight lifts as soft warmth spreads inside. I draw the words in deeper and then exhale them into every knotted cranny of my body. Could it be I am safe? Can I of all people really go there? Might I be welcome at long last? I can dip and twist, I can sway, wander and whirl. The melodies anchor me to my past while weaving a spiral staircase of new possibilities. My soul dances on waves of song, soaring to realms that have long awaited my homecoming. I do not need to read the words, for I have never forgotten them. They have been waiting to be reclaimed by my voice. I allow them to penetrate deep, to a wounded core where they might begin their healing.

I keep my eyes closed so that each song is another unseen partner in a new dance. The words dissolve and reform, reverberating with a thousand new meanings. *Ve'taher libainu l'uvdecha be'emet....* Purify. Heart. Worship. You. Me. Her. His. Our. Truth. What would it mean to land somewhere and to sink into the safety of knowing I am home?

On that first Friday night of my return, the silent prayer is followed by Rabbi Nachman's haunting melody about the very narrow bridge. *Kol ha-olam kulo* . . . all of the entire world . . . *gesher tsar me'od* . . . is a very narrow bridge, and the essential thing is not to fear anything at all. What might I fear? Perhaps the bridge is too narrow for my widely deviating path. Or I might fear that my own steps will falter before I can make it across the divide. Then there is the worst of my fears — that there may be nothing waiting for me even if someday I do reach the other side.

There were people, not always the most likely ones, who were guides along the way. Ron and Amy Guttman, a couple with whom we were friendly for years in Paris, were such people for me. They are a high-energy, fashionable pair, he a Belgian-born actor, he and she trend-spotting producers with an international reach. Our decades-long friendship had always centered around French adaptations of American scripts and discussions of reworking French creations for American tastes. Our concerns were theatrical, artsy, social, cosmopolitan, with our common Jewish roots surfacing only in passing, perhaps over the years, around the observance of Yom Kippur or the plans for one of my boys' bar mitzvahs.

One winter evening, before my moving back to New York or stepping foot in BJ, I brought a Paris-based North American friend to the Guttmans' art-filled Central Park West sanctuary for drinks. In typical fashion, my friend initiated some gossip about common acquaintances in the Franco-American entertainment world. Ron, however, would not take the bait. He politely explained that he did not indulge in gossip. There was a pause, a wordless moment. He explained that it had to do with avoiding something called *lashon ha'ra*, the evil tongue or harmful gossip, and how, since joining a certain congregation, he had determined to avoid it. It was a simple commitment to mindful speech, a shared communal value.

He said it casually, in a relaxed tone, but my friend needed a few minutes to take it all in. French society was barely imaginable without its steady diet of colorful gossip. As a child, I had been raised with the daily admonition to avoid *lashon ha'ra,* but it had been decades since someone had recalled that guideline. Ron had no way to know he was awakening a once-cherished dictum. I wondered what had gotten into him and how his membership in this community could provoke such a shift. I wanted not only to express admiration, but also to participate. He had found a way back across a long divide, and I thought for a moment that night, in spite of all my internal barriers, that perhaps I could, too.

Standing in the crowded BJ balcony that first Friday evening, I recall a detail from that night. When Ron spoke, I glimpsed the banner of the *Kol Hadash*, a publication of B'nai Jeshurun, placed on the coffee table, between the caviar and the iced vodka. The headline story was about the consequences of too-freely-spoken *lashon ha'ra.* In that moment I understand that crossing the bridge from one side to the other might simply be a matter of how consciously you take each step.

That Monday morning, I expect a call from the lawyer informing me of the date set for the dreaded deposition. She will surely want me to come down and start preparing with her for the nastiness of the inquisition. Instead she calls to say there is to be no deposition for now. Rather she is filing a Motion to Dismiss. According to the law, the issue of primary residency can only be raised at lease renewal time, and I am in mid-lease. For now, we have a sort of reprieve. No great optimist, she admits that due to the mid-lease technicality, my case looks a lot better to her than it did at first.

"The power of prayer," I breathe inaudibly into the telephone, only half believing it myself, nonetheless feeling for the first time a glimmer of hope.

The hearing is postponed for a month. I spend the intervening weeks back in France with E.T. and Jonathan, both of whom I sorely miss. When I unpack upon my return to the house in the French suburbs, I see that Raphael has dropped into my valise a CD of Sabbath songs recorded at Congregation B'nai Jeshurun.

I am now embarked on what turns out to be a two-year period of shuttling back and forth, with protracted legal wrangling, before I can definitively settle into my West Side apartment. First, the judge will grant us the motion, and the landlord's mid-lease challenge will be dismissed. Like an enraged troll, the landlord declares that he "has not yet begun to fight" and vows that he will "expose me in a decisive battle" come the expiration of my lease, fourteen months hence. He has no way of knowing I am a proud veteran of rage wars.

As predicted, I am in receipt of a Notice Not To Renew fourteen months later. If I lose my apartment, I will never be able to buy, burrow, or borrow my way back home. I am as determined as I have ever been about anything in my life that this not happen. Now I will surely have to prepare for a deposition proving my rights to residency. After that, we may or may not move to trial. It is going to be a long, hard, and very costly road. The landlord's resources are unlimited, while I am on the edge of a precipice. Without my mother's help, offered unconditionally (as opposed to my father, who would hold out money as a reward for religious concessions), I could not have prevailed.

I have a friend who is a retired five-star Israeli general. He explains that I am engaged in a war of nerves, that I need to find support systems to keep me strong while the other side resorts to everything legal and quasi-legal to destabilize my position. I take his advice to mean I need a solid spiritual grounding in a battle for personal survival. I also need a feeling of belonging so compelling that, like the defenders of Israel, I could not possibly, by legal sleight of hand, or financial attrition, or nervous exhaustion, be evicted from my turf. The congregation we call BJ gives me what I need at that time.

BJ draws me back again and again, although at the beginning, in that crowded place, I speak to no one, seek no friends, confide my fears to no one. I am needy but not trusting. After all, this place, graciously maintained by Jewish material wealth, might well contain more than its share of citizens who would side with the landlord and not with me. In pre-9/11 New York, and before the financial meltdown a few years away, New York City was still intoxicated with its own wealth, and the best and the brightest of the Jewish community were big players in this unregulated survival-of-the-fittest game. Avaricious Jewish men, financial speculators, landlords, and judges were posted like sentries with flaming swords barring my passage through the gates. Their greed finds justification in the law — after all, I had not occupied the contested apartment as primary resident for a long while. But I never cut ties or skipped a month's rent; I never missed an opportunity to visit nor ceased in my yearning. Clearly, the law of eternal return, callously defended halfway around the world in Israel by some of these same men, had no jurisdiction in the diaspora of milk and money. It would not be that difficult for them to condemn me into what this time would be irreversible exile.

For a two-year period, I spend one month in Paris and one month in New York in a determined campaign to bolster my primary residency claim. When I am back on the Upper West Side, thanks to Raphael and Ron, once a week, every week, I leave the stress of an impending eviction behind and enter the sanctuary of BJ. I rise with the others and pray for the health of a hopelessly ill friend. At a time of uncertainty, anguish, and woe, I long for the familiar safety of this music, for the solace of these ancient words. This re-immersion in my childhood restores faith that I can go home again. The psalms, with their promise of deliverance from distress, were written for me. I come for cleansing of the wounds that have long kept me from manifesting a home with strong foundations. I come for the aroma of fresh challah bread, for the *kiddush* cup held high, for the closing song that wishes peace to the coming and going of the angels.

*The masquerade holiday of Purim became a marker of the transi-*tional years between life in France and my resettling in New York City permanently at the end of 2001. In 1999, when I was straddling the two worlds, I overlooked the March holiday of Purim much as

I avoided the Hasidic stranger who approached Raphael and me in Washington Square Park to inform us of its celebration. One year later, however, though I still lived in France, I was once again visiting with Raphael in New York in March when he told me his salsa band had some kind of community gig on 88th Street between West End Avenue and Broadway.

It turns out that Raphael is part of an ad hoc salsa band hired to play for the all-out party that BJ is throwing for Purim this year. I hastily dress in an improvised costume of a 19th-century *raqs sharki* dancer, swathing myself in layers of veils and spirals of silver filigree belts, brightly colored waist scarves with multiple rows of jingling coins, and long earrings. I retreat to my balcony perch and watch as Rabbi Roly and his Argentinean coterie let loose to the salsa rhythms of my son's conga. From the balcony, I watch as Roly, taking my swarthy son for a native Spanish speaker, converses with Raphie for several minutes, with me feeling curious as I can be about their exchange. I am years away from introducing myself to this rabbi, whose intense kindness and particular intelligence are more than I can absorb in these early days of rapprochement. Later Raphie tells me that he let Roly know that although his Spanish was fluent, he was really a French Jew, that his mom was already a BJ member but for her own reasons was kind of shy.

The following year, March of 2001, we have just buried Lilah. I am about to fly down to Florida to pay a quick visit to my mother, who is prolonging her yearly stay in that warm clime. The day of my departure on Purim evening, I receive the news that the landlord has finally relented. My grueling, all-day deposition eight months earlier had been convincing enough that the landlord will not take me to trial. (My fear was that he would do so, not because he thought he could win, but only to bleed me dry.) He is dropping the charges and begrudgingly agreeing to give me a new lease. When I get down to West Palm Beach, I happily accompany my mother to her community synagogue to hear the *megilla* recount the victory of the few over the many, the underserved against the mighty. I thank Mom for all her support and let her know this same sort of victory is fully ours that day.

One year later, in 2002, my mom and I are alone in my apartment on Purim evening, as Raphael now has his own place in Brooklyn, Jonathan is studying in Montreal, and E.T. is traveling abroad as he often does. I have left France behind and now live full time in New York. Mom has lost all her hair from her chemo treatments and is too weak to walk in the street. I take one of my long veils and place it over her head and shoulders so that the sparkling gold lining flatters her face and eyes. Then I place a similar veil over my own head in a matching style. I push her in the wheelchair across the way to BJ to hear the *megilla* and watch the Purim play. She is as happy as a child, her boney fingers fluttering fancifully in the air, laughing and singing along with every one of the familiar tunes.

The next year, March 2003, I cannot bring myself to go to BJ on Purim. My mother has been gone only ten weeks, and though I suppose that even mourners are allowed to participate in the merriment of the day, my grief does not allow me to enter a house of raucous joy.

I wonder why Purim, more than any other holiday of the Jewish year, stands out as a marker of my journey. Purim is not one of the holidays prescribed from biblical times; rather, it arises from a communal urge to participate in the spring carnival festivals that were so widespread in Europe, particularly in Renaissance Italy. The Purim story, with its drunken revels, sordid politics, harem beauties, arrogant schemers, and foolish king could easily be trivialized, reduced to a pretext for the annual partying license issued to Jews at carnival time. There is no reference to God throughout the *megilla*, no Divine agency credited for any of the many turning points in the story. It is easy to conclude that whole affair is frivolous and contrived.

To counteract this tendency, Purim has been granted great prominence in the mystical tradition. There are those who say that in the messianic period, all Jewish holidays will be abolished with the notable exception of Purim; what's more, in the end of days, all sacred writing will disappear with the exception of the Five Books of Moses and Purim's *megilla*.

Purim remains non-abolished even in the messianic age because it has something very important to teach us: that behind the seemingly chaotic, occasionally unsavory, and often unwelcome events of our lives, there is indeed a Divine purpose. Even when it is least perceptible, all that looks random is a tapestry being woven by a Higher Intelligence. The moral of the story is that when we surrender to this insight, this same Higher Intelligence will, in its own way and in its own time, work out the kinks in our lives according to a loving and light-filled plan.

I confess that there is a Purim spark that has remained alive in me all along — that is to say, I harbor an intuitive reverence for some Unseen Force that has worked out some pretty impressive planning of my destiny. I would start with that one night so many years ago when in my mid-twenties I was seated next to a stranger on an arbitrarily chosen flight from New York to Paris. My seatmate and I had an easy rapport, though we did not exchange personal information. Still, a few days later I manage to run right into said random seatmate among the multitudes visiting the chateau of Versailles. My airplane buddy was accompanied by a young woman who insisted that I come to a dinner party that very night. And in the street on my way there, I met the man who became my husband, father of my children, and the central axis of my life — he, too, on the way to the same dinner party.

As far as I knew, I was just a tourist passing through Paris on my way to somewhere else. The Unseen Mover knew different. I had been determined to tour Versailles early in the day, but something irresistible had kept luring me back into a deep sleep. When I finally emerged in the early afternoon from disturbingly prophetic dreams, I caught a late train to Versailles. Once there, a strange woman handed me the address with the dinner invitation that would change the course of my life. A few hours later, E.T. and I, years and continents apart, with no known acquaintance in common, arrived at the fated location at the same moment, his Austin Mini cutting just in front of my idling cab. Like two chess pieces moved by the Benevolent Master, we stepped onto a sidewalk at dusk and met each other's glances.

That's a reassuring story, and it seems to have ended well, But I also see perfection of design when faced with adversity. Had not the New York City landlord, the Purim villain in my own life, threatened to evict me, I don't see how I would have generated the urgency to make it back to New York City (with no real enthusiasm on the part of E.T., with no defined plan and no means of financial support). If not for the impending lawsuit, would I have had my French household packed, my possessions sorted for shipment, my younger son Jonathan enrolled in the Manhattan French Lycée, when I suddenly learned of my mother's diagnosis of cancer? Something I cannot name conspired to have me there by my mom's side to see her through after all those decades away. And if I hadn't lost her so soon after burying Lilah, if Raphael had not been a disconcerting rebel, if my fight against the Powers That Be had not been so daunting, would I have found my way back to the synagogue we call BJ? Would I have returned there again and again with a doubting heart that was cracked open just enough to let in a Sabbath song?

There's something else about this marker holiday of Purim. It cautions you not to get carried away with metaphysical hubris. Now and then we manage to see our lives in what have been called "microdots," described by a man called Stoller as "the consciously experienced moments selected from the whole and arranged to present a point of view." But you are reminded that if/when you discern a Purim pattern connecting the microdots into a purposeful life story, it's time to drink yourself senseless, to get so wrecked you can no longer tell the difference between the evil Haman and the righteous Mordechai. After all, there are no fixed points, and, when pressed, the Forces at Play are jealous guardians of their secrets.

The Hidden Sphere

Part Three

A Women's Brigade

I am reeling, wishing I could get some fresh air quick. As I lean back in my chair, the room begins to spin. Avivah Zornberg teaches with a cultural range and psychoanalytic depth that draw me to her talks during her annual visit to New York City from Jerusalem. On this occasion, the leading female Bible scholar of our day interweaves a dizzying tapestry of ideas. But her main theme is the cruelty of God.

Dr. Zornberg softly but repeatedly utters the Hebrew word for cruel — *achzar*. Do we not agree that even the sound of it is harsh, dismissive? She then bisects the word to reveal an inner meaning: *Ach* means "indeed" or "only" and *zar* is Hebrew for "strange" or "alienated." This suggests an estranged God's inability (or stubborn refusal?) to empathize with the human heart.

I arrive at the Manhattan JCC venue moments before the admired visiting scholar comes up to the stage, and lucky for me, a woman who recognizes me from BJ ushers me to an available seat. The room at the JCC is filled to overflowing. As I listen, I'm overcome with confusion. It is not so much the intricacies of Dr. Zornberg's thought that make me dizzy as the thinker herself. Erudite, broadly cultured, gentle but unflinching, Avivah Zornberg is a woman of obvious emotional depth. Her manner is confident yet humble. She speaks knowingly of recognizable states — grief, longing, disappointment, even wild despair — but it is hard to imagine her experiencing these in an unrestrained way. Her speech is rapid, her voice is soft, distinguished by its clipped Scottish accent, and I have to listen closely to pick up on its unapologetic authority. She is not in an ivory tower nor does she pretend to be a commoner. Dr. Zornberg holds a Ph.D. in English literature from Cambridge University and rarely takes questions from her lay audiences.

What to me is most incongruent is the woman herself. Dr. Zornberg is a devout Orthodox Jew, a wife, mother, and grandmother keeping a relatively low profile in a close-knit Jerusalem community, leaving her home once a year to lecture for a few weeks in North America. So how does she teach that this version of God is *achzar*, estranged, indifferent, cruel, and still choose to remain faithful to the world order He and His male followers have contrived?

My perplexity aside, I'm holding on to every word she says. She is speaking about the despondent people of Israel who bemoan that they have been taken out of Egypt only to learn that their entire generation will not go up to the Promised Land. The people conclude that if this is their divinely decreed fate, it must be because God hates them. But then Dr. Zornberg wonders, along with Rashi, if this is not what we moderns would call projection, and is it not more likely that it is the people of Israel who, in this moment of limitless grief, hate God.

She considers the prospect of God-hating with marked evenness. She goes on to suggest that excessive cruelty on God's part may lead to undesired results on the human plane. I am astonished when I next hear her say, however softly, "God is, after all, at His best when He is not playing God." I expect the pillars of the room to start quaking and the community center roof to fall in at such bold words from one of the learned devout. The tremors seem to be taking place within my own entrails. This is advanced Judaism for thinking adults; Dr. Avivah Zornberg is a woman I must reckon with.

She speaks to her audience a few nights later about people who are stuck in a static way of viewing the world. She uses the word *gezera* to describe them. A *gezera* is a decree but, as Zornberg tells us, to be stuck in *gezera* mode is to dwell in Ezekiel's valley of dry bones, without the creativity, hope, or transformation that will someday let those bones live again. To be a victim of the *gezera* perspective is to say no to all possibility and to cling to the way things are. If you ask me, many a strictly Orthodox Jewish male is stuck in *gezera* mentality. My father lived in the shadow of *gezera*, with his outlook darkened by fears of impending doom justly deserved for falling short of God's standards. He simply could not see life in any other terms. Zornberg writes that to be limited by *gezera* mode is "to expire before redemption comes."

But we women, says she, are less likely to resign ourselves to such hopelessness. Women know that there is always a gradual ripening of even invisible moons; wombs shed their lining to clear space for new conception. In this talk, she is commenting on the Book of Exodus, on what it took for Jews to overcome not only Pharoah's *gezera* of doom but also their own limited mentality. It is the women who, counting on as-yet-unseen moons, reject *gezera* and then inspire the men to follow.

Even as a young girl, Miriam, the older sister of Moses, convinces her father to resume marital relations despite Pharaoh's decree that all male babies be drowned. When the Hebrew women seduce their withdrawn slave husbands, when the midwives defy Pharaoh's decree, when Miriam sets her infant brother afloat down the Nile and Pharaoh's daughter retrieves him, all these women challenge a fixed reality in order to make rebirth possible.

The anti-*gezera* force is unabashedly a women's brigade with Miriam in its fore. The women demand nothing less than a totally restructured way of looking at life. Thus, teaches Zornberg, begins our understanding of women's unconscious desire.

The Bible is frank in letting us know that this force can expect to meet with stubborn, and sometimes even violent, resistance. Moses is far from open to those who would call for the transformation of the *gezera* mentality. This kind of agitation is messy and full of risk. It demands that others reconsider their entrenched position. But women insist that if our story as Jews is to continue, we need a counter-force, a provocative disruption, a necessary polarity that defies for the sake of redemption.

The struggle between stasis and renewal that exists throughout the narrative of our people is a tension that inevitably weaves its way into our personal stories. With Zornberg's teaching, something in my self-perception shifts. Might adolescent rebellion be redefined as anti-*gezera* activism for change? When, in Exodus, Miriam convinces her father to act differently, the course of Jewish history is vitally altered. In my own way, I was trying to tell my father that his cherished outcome — the continued survival of the Jewish people — was best served by allowing for fluidity, by making room for each person's uniqueness. I was not able to convince my father that diversity could more vividly knit, rather than threaten, the fabric of the fold. How my whole life might have been different had I been able to persuade my father that my outer shell of defiance contained not only youthful rebellion but also a vital spark of anti-*gezera* renewal, in what Zornberg now ratifies as the finest tradition of uppity Jewish women.

Once repudiated, I took off, haunted by the fear of my own potential for wreaking havoc. I took off with the voice ringing in my ear that blamed me for a father's demise. He survived that first heart attack, but my relationship with my father and mother did not. Rage, I'm beginning to see, is a potent alchemy of grief and fear. There is grief that the vessel cannot contain all I am. There is fear that I will shatter the vessel. There is grief at a blessing denied. There is fear at hemorrhaging love. There is rage that the vessel — which is the whole Jewish worldview, with father as its central pillar and mother as the silently complicit deserter — cannot contain all that I grieve and all that I fear.

I find the courage to write to Avivah Zornberg and tell her something of my journey. In her prompt e-mail reply, Dr. Zornberg sends me her personal blessing. I sit for a while in silent gratitude for her generosity. What is a blessing if not a wish that the recipient be protected so that she or he might go on flourishing into who they really are? A blessing is a sanctification of its object, a ritualized wish that whatever is blessed may go on to express itself to the fullest according to its nature. "May God be with you just as He has always been with you from the moment of your birth until now." I remember how the blessing of the bat mitzvah girl wooed me over the BJ balcony, inviting me to tumble right into its force field. When I receive this reply from Dr. Zornberg, I consider a claim to a long denied birthright. I can imagine what it might be like to someday fully come into my own.

Round and Round

From where do all these stories come? We have extraordinary personalities such as Elijah, who will not overlook the question of a single soul when he returns as a harbinger of the Messiah. We envision angels dancing in a celestial circle around the wedding canopy of slaves when a little prescient girl convinces her father to remarry her mother and continue to procreate. We hear a disembodied voice, a *bat kol*, confirming the identity of a rabbinical heretic. We conjure two angels, a good and a bad, both of whom accompany us throughout the Sabbath day. We hear in detail of a prophetic vision of dry bones strewn across an arid terrain that will someday live again. From where, I increasingly wonder, does all this imagery come?

Zornberg has an answer for me. She is thoroughly informed by an acknowledgment of unconscious processes that are always at work. While perfectly coherent, Zornberg's explorations are not limited to the realm of rational thought. Rather she leads us into the limitless zone of religious imagination and encourages us to take back whatever resonates into our everyday lives. Zornberg reawakens my own attraction to an exploration of the unconscious, both for the dimension it brings to sacred texts and for the more personal purpose of healing old psychic wounds.

I enroll in a training course in advanced Ericksonian Hypnosis, and look forward to enriching my coaching skills with the healing power of the unconscious. Hypnosis is a technique for reconnection with whatever lies beneath the surface distractions of everyday life. It begins with induction into a trance state wherein we unlock images stored in our own repositories of insight and memory. Nothing could be more natural to our spiritual selves than turning within with heightened awareness. Little could be more empowering (and ultimately subversive) in a culture that keeps us enthralled with endless distractions.

Hypnosis is a first cousin to deep meditation, but without the stipulation of empty, content-less mind. Unlike classical meditation, hypnosis is most often a journey with a goal, be it to heal, to retrieve a resource, to re-imagine our childhood experience, or to project a helpful skill into a challenging situation. Hypnosis invites one's own unconscious to produce sensual imagery, encouraging visualization and language to spontaneously arise. It stands on the border between sleeping and waking life, and it has been used interchangeably with the term "waking dream." Some say that such elaborate schemas as the kabbalists' Tree of Life and Ezekiel's *merkava* or celestial chariot are likely products of hypnotic journeys, while some of the more imaginative forms of *midrash* might also well arise from trance.

I am about to embark on my first hypnotic journey as part of my training in Ericksonian hypnotherapy at a downtown institute. This is a healing journey in which the Older Self helps the Younger Self overcome some of the negative messages that have stunted her self-acceptance from early on. With her wisdom, the Older Self helps the Younger Self disarm the "alien thought viruses," that is, the critical messages with which every one of us was bombarded in our past. "Alien thought viruses" is a name that denotes that these negative messages are both external and self-propagating. The unwanted by-products of their invasion are a sense of inadequacy, disconnection, and unworthiness. The journey is a reliving of personal history so that each of us may grow up all over again, this time with birthright states (such as inner peace, wholeness, love, self-acceptance, connection, worthiness) available and intact.

A long-buried memory surfaces during my trance journey. It is a Sabbath day in late autumn, I am 13 or 14 years old, my devotion to a pious life is still as innocent as it is ardent. My mother has bought me a new outfit that gives me a kind of snappy, energetic feeling when I put it on. It is a tightly belted red vinyl jacket with a perky visor cap to match. With no destination in mind, I set off on a *shabbos* walk alone. Walking alone is unusual for me on the Sabbath. It is even more unusual that I would absentmindedly cross the crowded avenue where the elevated train clatters overhead and the Spanish immigrant neighborhood is clearly divided from the working-class-Jewish enclave where we live. I am wearing my first pair of heeled pumps; they are one inch high, and I like the confident clicking sound they make against the sidewalk.

I find myself on the other side of the avenue, feeling sprightly as I dreamily go through some outdoor racks of cut-rate lingerie and terrycloth slippers. I am concentrating on the words to "Wouldn't It Be Loverly" in the new Hebrew translation of *My Fair Lady*. I only realize I've been singing out loud when a small swarthy man sidles up to me and compliments me on my voice. He has a gold-plated front tooth. He adds that I have a pretty coat and cap along with lovely green eyes. I thank him with a friendly smile. Then, speaking in even lower tones, he tells me I am a very pretty girl. He likes my long dark hair and my fair skin. I have heard this before, sometimes even from strangers, but never spoken in quite so conspiratorial a tone. I am staring at his gold tooth, wondering if he is some kind of pirate, and I do not back away.

Then the man asks me in a whisper (I come a tad closer to hear) if I know that pretty young girls like me can make a lot of money in Manhattan. I don't know what he means. He then asks me if I know how to make a man happy. I think of how I make my father happy when I sing *shabbos* songs with him around the table or when I know all the lyrics to songs from *My Fair Lady* in Hebrew. I make my brother happy when I read books he recommends and give him my leftover chocolate pudding, and I make some boys in school happy when I lend them an extra pen and laugh at their silly jokes. So I nod to this small and swarthy man; I tell him yes. Naturally I know how to make a man happy.

Then he slips a little paper with a phone number into the pocket of my brand new *shabbos* jacket, telling me to call it whenever I am ready to come to Manhattan and make a man happy. He disappears into the racks of flower-printed housecoats, and I stand there not even daring to so much as touch the paper I now carry, the paper boring a hole into my hip. It is forbidden to tear paper on the Sabbath, and to throw it away I would have to touch it, something I cannot quite bring myself to do. I stand there and realize the holy day of rest is drawing to a close, and I have to cross back to the other side of the avenue and find my way home.

My Older Self now appears to guide my Younger Self to some kind of safety and understanding. The goal of the journey is self-acceptance and wholeness via revisiting some of the sketchier moments of the past. First, Older Self extends a hand and helps me cross the wide avenue. She does not speak until we are several yards away from the clattering overhead train. Wondrously, she knows exactly what I need to hear. Of course, she tells me, I have no idea why I smiled and came closer rather than backing away from the effrontery of this no-goodnik stranger. No, it does not mean I am corrupt at the core. She tells me that lots of young girls have a weakness for flattery; perhaps we intuit early on that success in charming men grants us whatever paltry leverage we might claim in a wide, unwieldy world.

She goes on to tell me that it's all to my credit that despite my cloistered upbringing I allowed myself to experience curiosity around something so foreign and unexpected. Now I feel she's being overly kind, but she insists that this openness, sagely directed, can serve me well, if only I would honor it. She senses the direction of my self-condemnation, although I say nothing. How, she asks me, could it possibly be my fault that I was raised with an unstinting eagerness to please men and no commensurate notion of the danger that such willingness implies? Such were the limits of the education available to me at the time. Yes, it's true that later on, growing up, these unchecked tendencies — the need to be desired, the compulsion to both destabilize and please — landed me in lots of places I would rather not have been.

My Older Self is here to remind me that back then I was unschooled and unguided, but now I have so many more choices. She urges me to expand my capacity for compassion to my young, unsponsored Self, just as she is doing right now.

This grown-up Self, she knows a lot. She can sense that I'm struggling with this, the first manifestation of the risk-taking, taboo-busting, danger-seeking part of myself, the part that compelled me to explore all manner of undergrounds for so many years. She tightens her reassuring grip around my thin shoulders. She tells me it's all part of the individuation process; it's made me who I am. I should applaud my bravery as an explorer of the shadow side; I am a more complete person, destined to be a better healer, maybe even a more complex writer, because of it.

So far, so good. Older Self tells me that I don't have to worry, she will now walk me all the way home and even accompany me upstairs for the *havdala* service marking the end of the Sabbath. During this time of year, we agree that it gets dark very early and it's not good to have to walk alone. She steadies my arm as I hold the braided *havdala* candle high while my dad chants in full voice of the separation of the holy and the profane, of the primordial divide between the hallowed and the unholy, she letting me know with a look that even when the melting wax singes my gripping fingers, it is not I who am separated out, not I who have lost my place in the domain of the sanctioned.

We pass around the filigreed silver spice box. Through the openings wafts the familiar aroma of cinnamon and clove. This is the sweet savor of Sabbath peace. A line from Whitman's "Song of Self" comes to my mind as I inhale deep: "I breathe the fragrance Myself and know it and like it."

The scene dissolves, and for a few unsettling moments my Older Self vanishes. I am on an empty stage feeling the black terror of utter aloneness. I have abandoned the right path and I am to be abandoned in turn. Women, and those raised in traditional homes in particular, have their own gender-based version of this pernicious viral encoding. If we do not accept the given order, we cut ourselves off forever from anyone who can help us. This comes about because the evil inclination has taken us over from within; it happens because we are not pure, strong, and devoted enough to overcome. In my tradition, it starts early on; after all, women are born impure from the uterus of another woman. A woman's internal reality is early on invaded by the alien censure of a masculine God; the bloodstain of female ungodliness is not easy to dissolve.

My Older Self reappears to encourage my Child Self to let go of the old story, all of the old stories. She whispers to me in Hebrew — *ah na el na, refah na la* — it is time for all this to be healed with fresh Divine energy. Then she holds me in her arms and rocks me just as my mother used to when, on so many nights, I sobbed in despair over not yet having breasts, of having no sign from a withholding God that I would ever be a real woman. *Ve'az titrapeh* . . . then she shall be healed. She offers me pure compassion as she — Older Self, Younger Self, Miriam, Avivah, Mother and Chochma the Wise Woman — hold the space of my tears.

She and I sit together now side by side. We could be on a bench in the playground just across from my childhood house. There's lots of shouting and scuffling and ball-batting all around, but we are inside our own cocoon. My feet do not quite meet the ground when I sit on the bench, but I know it's okay to dangle. I grow calm as our identities merge. All that we are and always have been now shines unsullied. Mine is a rewrite of internal programming on the most profound level. We Are What We Are and always have been. We manifest blessing from the scabs of a curse.

Just as I am about to end my journey, I flash on an image familiar to me from dreams. My father, mother, maternal grandparents, my brother and I, my younger self and older self are holding hands and circling in a round dance. We are no longer subject to the pull of gravity, our circle dance levitates on some kind of celestial cloud. It is a magic circle, a sacred enclosure of union and reconciliation. All the petty differences have dissolved. We are reunited in harmony and acceptance. Our bond is not to be severed; it is as unconditional as eternity, abolishing all that came before; we are bathed in the radiance of the Source, and we circle round and round.

Anochi

I am surprised to see Rabbi Roly pause at our row and make eye contact with me. I have never been formally introduced to him, nor does my extreme illness-of-ease around male rabbis (yes, still) allow me to simply introduce myself. The gregarious E.T., present at BJ with far less emotional vulnerability than I, enjoys a sporting banter with the polyglot rabbi. But light social exchange with male religious leaders just doesn't come easily to me.

This was an exceptional Friday night about a year and a half after I had permanently resettled on the Upper West Side. Not only E.T., but also Raphael and Jonathan and Raphie's then girfriend Jodi accompanied me. We are seated one next to the other downstairs, near the outside aisle. I don't recall why we ventured downstairs or what the occasion was, perhaps a marking of serendipitous family togetherness during which everyone agreed to take an hour out and join Mom at her latest neighborhood hot spot.

When Roly stops at our row, I think surely he has come to arrange drum lessons with Raphie or discuss a soccer score in French with E.T. or make the acquaintance of our lovely young lady or congratulate Jonat on his recent return from humanitarian work in Bangladesh. But as it happens, he has come to have a word with me. I am the very same Susan Reimer-Torn who's written about Ruth in a certain anthology, am I not? Yes, indeed, I am she. I am amazed when he asks me to be one of three speakers to teach about the biblical figure of Ruth at the upcoming all-night study session that marks the holiday of Shavuot.

I am as astonished to be chosen as I have been indignant at being overlooked. But my amazement extends beyond my surprise at the discovery of my article and Roly's going out of his way to identify its author. I am in a state of radical awe about the timing. Unknown (or so I assume) to anyone else, I am on this particular Friday night contending with a fierce bout of self-rejection. The internal soundtrack that I know by heart, which nonetheless lays me grievously low, goes something like this: How have I managed to waste my life so irredeemably? I am a woman who squandered her early education, who broke her father's heart, who failed to keep up with a whole thriving community of contacts, who never managed to distinguish herself among her Jewish peers. I have failed to make any sort of mark in a world that long ago might well have welcomed my contribution. Now it is surely too late. What's worse, I have estranged my own two boys from their Jewish heritage, and due to my poor choices there may be no future Jewish generations issuing from my loins.

I have since come to know that BJ's Rabbi Roly is one of those rare spiritual leaders whose finely honed intuition leads him to say just the right thing to people and at the moment when they need it most. On that Friday night, my sense of I, my *anochi*, was particularly weak, and Roly, knowingly or not, was piercing through a thicket of painful self-condemnation.

I will get up there on Shavuot, night of cosmic revelation, because this man whom I hardly know has asked me to. Apparently he came across my piece and considers it worthy of a congregational teaching. That is another subject of wonder. The angle on the Ruth story that the piece explores is far from mainstream. This published essay was inspired by a conversation I had once upon a time with my friend Hesh, who had spoken to me, of all things, of the paradox of Ruth — questioning in his low, suggestive voice how and why a woman whose ancestry is sown in incest comes to be the bearer of the Davidic messianic seed. Ruth is not only a stranger, she is from the pariah tribe of Moab, forbidden to Jews in marriage because of their unsavory origins in father-daughter incest. It is in Ruth that redemption, our highest aspiration, is preserved in the outer shell of a heinous taboo. What's more, Hesh pointed out, Ruth is positioned midway between transgression and salvation: There are seven generations leading back to her tribal inception in incest, and seven generations going forth to the birth of King David. Why is she placed squarely in between these two extremes? What lesson might we draw from the Bible's ascribing an incest-tainted lineage to the female forebear of Israel's ultimate redeemer? My edgy essay found its place in print among others authored by women with far more scholarly credentials than I.

Shavuot is the holiday when we recite and contemplate the biblical Book of Ruth. It seems Roly is encouraging me to stand up in front of his congregation, to take my place between two rabbis at some magical hour just before the stroke of midnight, and on this night of revelation, to reveal my particular take on a woman of a despised tribe who is singled out as a foremother of the Messiah. Has Roly, I wonder, actually read the essay? Does he realize that I see Ruth as a transformative field, a figure in which the highest and lowest, a highly charged taboo and ultimate redemption, are reconciled? I have no idea what he knows. But I do know I will get up there and address the congregation with an unusual teaching that is strongly resonant with me, because he has invited me to do so.

It so happens that both my boys, Raphael and Jonathan, are in New York City for this event, as is Raphael's girlfriend, Jodi. While they know that BJ is becoming increasingly important to me, I rarely involve them in the sort of esoteric conversations that I often entertain and sometimes write about. Even less do I use coercive tactics to get them to join me at services: Much as I long for them to come, I will not re-enact anything that reminds me of my own parents' always-anxious insistence. Somehow, though, it matters much to me that they come to this late-night lecture; I want my family to be present for an event that marks my first teaching on a Jewish holiday to a synagogue gathering. It is not important if they engage with the subject, but I want them to witness me in this old/new context. And yes, I dream that my re-engagement with Jewish tradition will someday be something we all share and eventually pass down, uninterrupted, to future generations.

I take my place and I speak out loud. My voice does not tremble; I am rooted in what I have to say. I nod to my friend Joseph who as always is stationed in the front-row aisle seat. I explain that way back in grade school when I first met Ruth, she was never one of my favorite biblical personae. To be frank, she was a bit of a turn-off. Young, widowed, and childless, Ruth puts aside all concern for herself in deference to Naomi, her bereaved mother-in-law. Ruth's generosity and loyalty were, of course, admirable, but deep down I was resentful of womanly worthiness measured in degrees of self-sacrifice. My distaste for self-abnegation led me to dismiss Ruth. In retrospect, it blinded me to what I now see as her startling subversive dimension. Happily, it's never too late to reconsider.

I look up and try to gauge the interest level of the audience. Scores of expectant, curious, engaged faces look back at me. Jodi is transfixed in admiration; the boys look a tad more skeptical. After talking more about the text, and about women who prefigure Ruth in both the Bible and other mythological traditions, I end on a personal note. Along with many Orthodox girls, I was educated with relentless emphasis on the dichotomy of right and wrong, virtue and vice, the light of faith versus the darkness of doubt. There were good girls (who were not vain or selfish) and not-such-good girls (who were both). I never did well within those dualities. But now it seems that this sort of meeting of radical opposites is the very process our tradition repeatedly, if subtly, points to as a necessary ingredient in the making of a Messiah.

When I conclude, Joseph shouts out, *"Ya'asher ko'akh,"* a Hebrew equivalent of *"Brava."* When I look up, E.T., Jodi, and my sons are flashing me broad grins. I look around for Roly, but I'm not sure where he's gone.

It is once again the late springtime holiday of Shavuot, three years after my own late-night talk on the paradoxical provenance of Ruth. Inquiries into Ruth draw me back again and again; chances are I will stay up late again this year to hear what others have to say.

It is 1:00 in the morning, and those of us who have decided to stay are padding down the stairs to the BJ basement feeling dutiful and daring. There is an undercurrent of excitement among the crowd on the stairs, an after-hours buzz, as if we are young again and waiting for the late-night appearance of a reclusive rock star or subversive anarchist poet. Shavuot is the night culminating the Omer, a period of seven weeks devoted to personal refinement, the night when from pagan times it is known that the stars are aligned for revelation. On this particular Shavuot, the BJ buzz is all about one Rabbi David Silber; it is agreed that he is well worth waiting up for into the wee hours. A friend asks excitedly if I have ever heard Silber speak.

For me, that's not a straightforward question. As it happens I have heard David Silber speak — or struggle to — many times, but never as an adult, never as a teacher of seekers who throng to hear his words in the wee hours. In the Beforetime — or was it another lifetime? — David and I both sat countless times at his mother's carefully laid table, where the silver shone and the glasses sparkled and everything was strictly in its designated Sabbath place. His mother, Martha, and my mother, Mildred, were lifelong best friends. Our two families lived just across the street from one another, and throughout my childhood we shared the details of daily life as well as the dimension of religious observance. Martha would buy the koshered chickens, and a bashful David would deliver the extra one to our door. Mom would buy the challah loaves, and I would deliver the Silbers' to their door. Martha, like my mom, was indefatigable, strictly non-self-indulgent, and a dedicated public school teacher. Unlike my mom, she was a compulsive housekeeper. She stopped in her chores only long enough to meet me at the door with the standard greeting: "Working hard?" I didn't know how to answer. (How hard was hard enough?) But I had no doubt that Martha was more than fulfilling the requirement.

Yes, I have heard David speak, or try to, back in the days when his mother despaired over his refusal to eat a raw vegetable, and his words came out like repetitive machine gun fire, starting strong and jamming up in a bottleneck of sounds. I remember asking my mother in a whisper, over at our end of the long rectangular table, why it was that David stuttered. She explained that his mind worked much faster than his tongue possibly could. Back in those childhood days, David was the go-

114

to guy among the boys for his encyclopedic knowledge of baseball stats. Summers when our families vacationed in the same Catskill bungalow colony, he would give in to his mother's insistence that he stop reading and join us in the lake. He would wade in knee-deep, hoping that we would be considerate enough not to splash the pages of the cherished book he held high and dry in his hand.

Rabbi David Silber has founded a revolutionary Orthodox school for women, won many awards, and fathered eight children with a wife named Devora who's started yet another school and won still more awards. I assume that by now Rabbi Silber's tongue has somehow caught up with his high-velocity brain — and that from time to time on a hot summer day, as long as it is not too close to the fast day of Tisha B'Av, he even deigns to take a dip.

It is just shy of 2:00 in the morning in the all-night study session known as *tikkun leil shavuot*. I'm deliberating whether or not I will go over and say hello to the son of my mother's lifelong best friend. Why would I not? Well, for starters, he is a distinguished rabbi and I'm a runaway; he has a long list of stellar achievements and I have simply cut loose, contributing little. But when will I get over whatever is left of the vestigial shame and self-rejection that boils up whenever I am in the presence of those from my past who never strayed? I am, for heaven's sake, a visibility coach to other women. Why can't I present my greetings to David, ask after the health of his mother, who, now in her nineties and living in Israel, was a formative figure of my youth? I look over his way, daring myself to simply be present with whatever his greeting might be. There is something insolvent clinging to me inside, a self-imposed, paralyzing *gezera* preventing me from coming forth.

It is now past 2:00, and we are on a refreshment break. Jews ward off sleep with an endless supply of lukewarm coffee and cheesecake. A small, dark man with closely cropped hair and a giant *yarmulke* covering his skull, David is sitting on a chair with his eyes closed, wrapped in his own cocoon, rocking back and forth, mouthing some words of prayer or self-preparation or communion with Spirit or rehearsal of the talk he will soon give. I am off the hook; this is not the right moment for a social call.

A few minutes later, when I join the short line for hot tea, I lift up my eyes and there he is, Rabbi David Silber, with his wife Devora by his side, just a few feet away from where I stand. "Hello David," I manage to say, after taking a step in his direction. He looks confused; the flicker of recognition is not strong enough to distinguish me from the legions of petite, middle-aged Jewish women who have over these many years flocked to his classes, contributed to his worthy cause, entrusted him with their promising daughters. I do not allow the awkward moment to drag on. "I'm Susan Reimer," I say simply, and he smiles, more from relief at my solved identity than any distinct pleasure in my reappearance.

Quickly, I ask after his mother's health and learn that she is no longer mentally competent. I cannot imagine Martha going gently into the night of despondent confusion. I remember how in the days before her *aliya* to Israel, which corresponded with my mother's chemotherapy, Martha despaired of the way the chemicals had reduced my mother's heretofore full capacity to retain information. Martha evinced no patience for endless repetition, even for the benefit of her closest friend. Now she was off in Israel, living near her daughter, her youngest son, and her tribe of grandchildren, and feeling disoriented, uprooted, useless, and lonely. I share a sigh with the rabbi, a sigh full of helpless regret for better days gone by.

Then David introduces me to his wife Devora, who is revered in her own right as an inspired teacher and founder of a Jewish elementary school. I remember when she first came into David's life, and a fault-finding Martha shared her concern with my mom: Devora was so impossibly skinny, could she even get pregnant? Now, some thirty-five years and eight children later, she is still impossibly skinny, abstemious, wearing no-nonsense shoes and carrying a canvas backpack, without a stitch of make-up or a hint of personal adornment. Devora greets me with a welcoming smile. She looks at me and says, *ah yes,* she sees something of my mother's expression around my eyes. She has vivid memories of my mother's weekly *shabbat* inclusion at Martha's table in the many years when Mom was a widow and I was somewhere else, nothing more than a ghost of a memory to those ingathered there.

Devora graciously comes up with a tribute to Mom. It seems my mother had a special way of communicating with one of Devora's children. I think of my mom's sweet warmth, her cultivated skill as an elementary school teacher; I grieve over the many ways her mothering passed me by.

The week before I was to leave France for good, I received an e-mail informing me of my mother's diagnosis. It was thoroughly alarming, and I had no clear idea of what lay ahead. She had never been sick before. Still, relief mitigated my despair. I was already packed and on my way home. Whatever support Mom would need in time of illness, I would no longer be an ocean away.

In the months before her death from multiple myeloma, my brother Joseph and I moved our mother into the Esplanade, a senior residence in the West 70s just off Riverside Park. E.T. and I and three of her grandchildren spent lots of time there, managing until the final weeks to eclipse any preoccupation with devastating illness.

The chemo treatments dulled my mother's otherwise sharp mind, meaning that she was never entirely clear how sick she was, how long she would stay in "the hotel," as she called the Esplanade. (We convinced her she was just away on vacation to spare her the daunting task of clearing out her apartment of over fifty years).

I would walk down to the Esplanade on Friday nights and wheel my mother some ten blocks up West End Avenue to BJ services. She would enter a state of rapture and was given to forgetting that I had ever turned my back on all this, indeed, that I had ever moved away. (She was more than once surprised to hear me conversing with my children in French; she had forgotten that they were raised there.) I once remarked to my brother that I was sure our father, who died in 1984, would be delighted by this turn of events. My brother was not so sure. After all, at this congregation, men and women sit together, musicians play on *shabbos*, the words of the liturgy have been changed to include such things as the names of the foremothers along with the fathers, women read from the Torah and share all religious duties with men in an atmosphere that some are calling post-gender. Perhaps my brother was right about our father. But BJ had so sweetened my experience that now and then I managed to forget about all the others out there who would rush to condemn it.

Before the weather turned sharply cold in autumn of 2002, I would bundle up Mom's shrinking body in a warm coat, cover her with a blanket, and wheel her out to Riverside Park. We would go to a promontory on 72nd Street overlooking a wide expanse of the Hudson. The Jersey Palisades coastline curves in a little at that spot, giving the whole an embracing crescent feel. I would help Mom out of the wheelchair so she could look over the low, stone wall and take in the scene along with the iodized marine air. All of life seemed to crack open for us in that fleeting, glistening moment. This was the last outdoor ground we ever stood together, the last earthly landscape we shared.

When I was a little girl, my mom and her mother, my grandmother Clara, often called me *Mamele*. It means "little mommy," or, if you will, mommy-to-be, an assignation of role and responsibility that will never lighten or expire.

There was one day just before the Rosh Hashanah holiday in the months before her death, when the weather was still balmy and Mom and I sat on a bench beneath a late-blossoming tree. I am wearing a wide floppy hat, a ruffled skirt, platform shoes, and oversized leopard-print sunglasses. E.T. comes to join us, and remarks on my get-up: "Susan always wanted to be a glamorous star," says he. My mom turns to me admiringly and says, "It's not too late." We all laugh, and she repeats herself as she was wont to do in those days. "It's not too late for you, *Mamele*, and I mean that, too." Did she mean for me or for us?

In those final months with my mother, we never discussed past differences, we never asked for an accounting or belabored the many ways that we had disappointed each other. She never asked me to explain why I had chosen to live so far away. I never asked her why she had abandoned me to my father's wrath and terrible accusations. I felt a certain tenderness for this brave, cheerful, undemanding, aging woman coping with her illness with great dignity. I had difficulty fully connecting her with the mother of my youth. I did not forget that in many ways she had not supported my coming of age, that years went by when we found no way to enrich one another's lives as two grown women. I knew that each of us had been able to do this for other people, even across generations, but that some channel of trust and communication between us had been clogged. I was there for her because I wanted to be, and because she needed me to be, and because it seemed clear to me that I was meant to answer this call before I could entirely reclaim the fullness of a New York life. I was not able to find a deep, personal connection to her, but something in me was wise enough not to insist upon it.

Instead, and for the first time since the rupture, Mom and I were able to share simple, daily things with one another in a manner that I imagined other mothers and daughter routinely did. We figured out where she might get her hair done when it grew back snowy white after chemo, and what kind of clothes we should buy now that she was shrinking several sizes. We sorted through delicacies at Zabar's sharing our favorite indulgences, she for once not needing to worry about putting on too much weight, I taking on that concern for the first time. We talked about my boys' divergent interests and possible directions for their futures, with me always minimizing the very real possibility that Raphael would consecrate his life to music rather than law, medicine, or nuclear physics. I would come over some afternoons when the Esplanade showed a classic film, and we would laugh over a little piece of nonsense until she fell asleep. I would reassure her that she hadn't forgotten anyone's birthday and that the nice people who looked after her at the Esplanade were being properly compensated.

There was one topic we never discussed, no matter how subtly or boldly I attempted to broach it. My mother never once in her eighteen final months said anything at all about the nearly forty years of her life that she had spent with my father. By then he had been gone for eighteen years. My brother confirmed my observation when he came to visit. If we asked her something about our dad, she would get a blank look and just let it slide, changing the topic, as if a reference to him had nothing to latch onto in her slippery memory stream.

She had experienced several different phases in the eighteen years since Dad's sudden death from a fatal heart attack. Mom started wintering in Florida, socializing with different sorts of people, even making the acquaintance of an adoring suitor, a man whom, ten years after my dad's death, Mom had the courage to marry in a Jewish ceremony, though never in a civil one. Unlearned, not very observant, this man made her happy in ways my father never could. After she buried her second husband, her only real love, she still had a few good years before she suddenly became ill.

My most outstanding memory of those final months is how my mother's face would light up whenever I came to see her. No matter how often I came, she couldn't take for granted that I was there by her side. *"Mamele!"* she would call out to me with delight as she awoke from a catnap in an upholstered lobby chair. As the weeks went by, she began forgetting more and more things. But she always recognized me, even from afar, and her light of unconditional love never wavered. It was a beam of sheer loving energy that grew stronger every day. I liked to be with her because of the unconditional acceptance she came to radiate, I liked the way it abolished history and rooted me in the present. As she grew closer to death, the experience grew less personal and more universal and, in some strange way, no less satisfying for its transcendence of personal narrative.

During the last weeks of Mom's life, my brother Joseph and I took turns with full-time nurses to keep her as comfortable as we could in her room at the Esplanade. Every morning, her linen was soaked with blood, a side effect of her cancer. We would do our best to wash her and the linens, providing constant changes of clothes and towels, hoping that the management would not insist we move her to a hospital. Finally, we made hospice arrangements and awaited the inevitable.

On that last Friday night of her life, I helped her light her Sabbath candles. She and her two candles were frighteningly wobbly, and I stayed for hours, making sure that she and her lights made it through the night. There was a story I wanted to tell her. I do not know if she followed the narrative as I told her about Pablo, who, so many years ago, in the period of my estrangement, had come to visit us in Paris. He had found his way, along with the errant angel from her own story, to our Sabbath table. Mine was the story of a little black boy who glimpsed a sanctuary in time, a story of a moment at which Sabbath was a mother and that mother was me. But I was, and always will be, no matter where I roam, daughter of my own mother, who now lies slowing dying along with her Sabbath lights.

When I manage to inform David, "I am Susan Reimer," I think of Ruth in the field, her irregular behavior also set in the middle of the night, when she lays herself down in the the threshing room at Boaz' feet. Her remote kinsman awakens and is not at all clear who this woman is. She says simply, "*anochi* Ruth," "I am Ruth," but her meaning is bold. Her *anochi*, her "I," is modest but confident. Avivah Zornberg tells us, "if the *anochi* is of a certain quality, everything else follows."

In these many ways, I am sorry to say I am not Ruth. She is a much-extolled clinger, someone whose attachment, even to a people she has never really known, cannot be dissuaded. I am an escape artist, a defector; I am Suzi Maybe Not Such a Good Girl. I earned the title when I was 15 and ventured for the first time to the decaying side street where Lilah lived with her dour and dutiful Aunt Flora.

Lilah, whose own mother left her an orphan, languished in a kind of Jewish-Germanic gloom in a railroad flat kept tidy by her humorless refugee aunt. It was my idea and I had already tried it out, seeing myself as a liberator, a champion of the avant-garde: We would go ice-skating in Central Park on a Sunday afternoon, out in the open with strangers. Like them, we would revolve in aimless circles to music without a hint of gravitas. Lilah could rent skates, and like me, she would first hold onto the sides for dear life. Then, gradually, she would make forward strides, mastering the weight-shifting slide, never straying too far from the periphery but steadily gaining momentum until, eventually, we would be gliding round and round, if not exactly with a dash of glamor then at the very least with an air of insouciance.

I raced up the five flights of stairs, wary of the odor emanating from Lilah's graffiti-sprawled lobby. I was dressed in a manner I deemed befitting avant-garde forays in urban adventure: There were two red pompoms affixed to the tips of my skates while a matching ornament was coquettishly positioned on the rim of a plaid beret.

I rang the doorbell several times while someone eyed me suspiciously through the peephole. It was only when I heard Lilah twice sing out, "It's Suzi!" that the door partially opened. Looking warily from me to her breakaway charge, Flora put down her dust mop and mused for all eternity: "This Suzi . . . I think she is . . . maybe . . . not such a good girl."

Lilah and I raced down the grime-coated staircase. The blade of my skates punctuated each step with a cutting thump against my breastbone. Together we exulted in Flora's heavily accented observation. Her Germanic speech weighed down every word and insured a ponderous space between them. "Maybe not such a good girl" was a distinction bestowed, an earned badge of courage, an honorific that for better or for worse would always stick.

My *anochi* is wobbly, plagued with doubt, willing to take one small step out and then hurriedly to retreat many steps back again. But come to think of it, there is perhaps one way I am like Ruth: Like her, I have come to redeem a questionable past.

As I stay into the wee hours of the all-night study session, seated on the carpeted floor, cross-legged, barefooted, wrapped in blankets, stomach grumbling, I gradually open to a free-associating mind, a non-linear, knowing mind more susceptible to the whispers and hints of revelation. It is, no doubt, to achieve this state that we forfeit sleep and allow ourselves to open to new ideas on this night. My drowsy free-flowing mind reels back to what Avivah Zornberg said about the vow that forefather Jacob made when he, too, left his parents' home and went into exile. Jacob swore that he would return to "his father's house" in peace. But the truth of the matter, Zornberg tells us, is that the expression, "father's house," is a reference to his mother, for it is a mother who founds and inspires the house of the father. So Jacob has sworn to return to his mother — a vow, it turns out, he cannot keep.

Jacob returns home after twenty-two years away. At 4:00 in the morning, my eyes barely open, the common length of our exile startles me. I, too, was away for twenty-two years. Jacob starts home because his mother, Rebeccah, has sent a wet nurse named Devora to tell Jacob it is time to return. Sadly, this elderly Devora dies on the return trip home. Jacob buries her and weeps without restraint. The commentators tip us off — when grief is excessive, it is often masking an unexpressed grief for someone else whose loss is so devastating that we cannot even bring ourselves to directly mourn it. We know that Jacob does not get home in time to see his mother alive. We learn very little about Rebeccah's death; it does not even rate a mention in the biblical text.

Zornberg, who on this night is present only in my mind, explains that Jacob was never able to process his feelings for the woman who had such a great influence on his life yet whose inner core he has never known. That woman was Rebeccah, Jacob's mother. She sends him Devora to bring him home, just as, posthumously, my mother has sent me a woman of that same name, now that I am home. This Devora, my Devora, who is married to David Silber, so often sat by my mother's side. Throughout the years I was gone, she kept Mom company at the *shabbat* table and sang with her the soulful Sabbath songs. I was elsewhere, living out my twenty-two years away. Devora admired my mother's professionalism as a teacher, and even gleaned from her some insights into the rearing of her own kids. Like Jacob, I always intended to come home to father's house — that is, to my mother — with some kind of wholeness. Although, unlike Jacob, I did return eighteen months before my mother's death, and although there was some closure in that time we finally spent together, I do not pretend to have known her nearly as well as this Devora did.

Devora is intimidating in her abstemious, unswerving piety, but in the weeks that follow, I sometimes find myself sitting close to her, often behind, always without a word, hoping that by drawing near I may approach the still-unsolved mystery of my mom.

A Vial of Myrrh

Dr. Zornberg has asked me to introduce myself to her when she comes for her North American lecture tour in the spring. I arrange my schedule to be able to attend several of her talks in the New York and Boston areas. I walk uptown through Riverside Park on the evening of her first talk at the Union Theological Seminary. The park is a riot of spring blossoms; at one section I walk through a corridor of pink cherry blossoms, inhaling sweet savor with every step.

I climb out of the park and hurry along to the august building that will house her talk, managing, as is my weakness, to arrive a few moments late. I slip into a seat in the back row and consciously exhale long, the better to let go of my moorings, the better to drift into the stream of consciousness awakened by this long-awaited speaker.

That evening, Avivah Zornberg is embroidering upon the biblical tale of Joseph and his brothers, their cruelty to him, his unheard cries of anguish when they throw him into the pit. She speaks of Joseph's long alienation from his family, and even more strikingly, his estrangement from his own inner life throughout the years of his initiation journey. Dr. Zornberg guides us through the story of this ruptured family's reunion years later, when Joseph rises to second in prominence to Pharaoh, and his older brothers are needy supplicants fleeing a famine in their native land. I surrender with delight to the flow of her narrative, its many currents.

Although I've agreed to introduce myself after the talk, still, I hesitate. She and I are not a likely pair. In Jewish tradition, an indelible demarcation line runs through the heart of our daily lives: There are foods that are kosher and others that are not; the Holy Sabbath is separated from the profane days of the week; in Orthodox gatherings, there are men and, on the other side of the divide, there are women.

Among the women there are good girls and there are also some who are, shall we say, not so obviously good. Avivah Zornberg is a woman of great valor, and despite the blurring of polarities suggested by Ruth, it remains clear to me on which side of the fence I belong.

I overcome my cramping reservations and approach her. I am dressed with uncharacteristic modesty, but I am toned and tanned from a recent vacation, while she is soberly garbed in navy blue, and moving slowly. I cannot hide — nor, perhaps, should I attempt to — my breakout from Orthodox norms. We are on opposite sides of the Great Divide. I say a few words and, feeling ill at ease as is my wont, I move away. I am confronting my very own tightly knotted *gezera*, a self-condemning edict that will not be so easily undone.

It would be unfortunate if after our written exchanges, I cannot find a way to approach her — for in her telling of the Joseph story, she has touched me in my core.

When Joseph's brothers throw him into a pit leaving him to his fate among the scorpions, they are deaf to his cries. Finding no echo in the world of family, Joseph becomes estranged even from his own inner life. The twenty-two-year rupture with his past, the "oblivion" he seeks while a high-achieving stranger in Egypt, reminds me of the twenty-two years I spent in France in self-imposed exile from my family of origin.

Later on, under extreme duress, his older brother Judah approaches Joseph on his magisterial throne. *Va-yigash Yehuda:* Judah draws closer and is finally ready to speak his own truth. Both men have suffered from unmet needs for connection, and from deadening emotional constraint. In the moment of his own soul-baring, Judah breaks through his brother's defenses. And in the midst of all this terrifying disclosure, Avivah Zornberg assures us, the long-darkened light of spirit once again illuminates Joseph's face.

Sitting and listening to her in the back row, I know what it takes to draw closer to intimates after many years away, how terrifying it is to approach the naked truth of unfinished drama, how overwhelming it can be to acknowledge the still-nagging need for love. I know, as she does, that this is no let's-make-up-and-live-happily-ever-after tale.

It is, rather, a scarred-forever story of misgivings, rupture, and tentative rapprochement.

There is a reception after her talk, affording me another opportunity to approach Dr. Zornberg. I speak simply. I tell her that of all the stories of the Bible — yes, really, of all of them — the Joseph story has always evoked in me the greatest emotion. But, I tell her, drawing a tad closer, until this evening, I have never understood why. At last I can be present with the personal meaning it has for me. She looks at me with silent understanding. For a few moments we hold one another's glance, eye to eye, enjoying a slower, quieter breath, a moment of possibility, of seeing one another in a whole new light.

I take my courage into my hands and invite Dr. Zornberg to lunch on the afternoon of her final evening talk in New York. To my delight, she makes time for a one-on-one encounter. There is something light and girlish in her gait as she appears in a wide-brimmed hat, flowing summer dress, and light cardigan. It is as though we are about to sit down to a lighthearted picnic on the grass. We choose a quiet table in one of the Upper West Side's strictly kosher eateries.

I follow her to the small sink where we use a tin cup attached to the wall by a linked chain to ritually wash our hands, spilling water first on the right, then on the left, three times each. We are silent until we recite the *hamotzei* over the bread. We begin with warmth and unfamiliarity. I tell her that I spent twenty-two years in France, and while I admire her frequent weaving in of Lacanian references, I confess how difficult it was for me to live among the post-modernists.

She has been reading my blogs, she knows my story of alienation from and tentative return to Jewish life. Before we part, Avivah asks me a very important question. She asks it kindly, the way you might inquire of the progress, both personal and academic, of a hopeful student. She wants to know if I have forgiven or reconciled with my father, if only in my mind after his death.

Everything is compressed into that moment: my longtime resentment of the wrathful God, the fulminating father who refused me his blessing, the fathers who spit in the uplifted faces of their provocative daughters, the beckoning stranger with the golden tooth, Joseph's eyes shining through the thickening fog. I see Lilah and me opening our mouths for that first taste of forbidden food, and I see Lilah's coffin being lowered into the ground, after which I am banished by black hats to the hinterland of my own apartment. I memory-scroll to the esteemed rabbi of my childhood beating his son Hesh within an inch of his life because the boy had tricked God into letting him live while taking his older brother. I flash on Miriam clawing at her diseased face, and the Acher galloping past the *shabbat* boundaries, waving his disciple back, while God desperately calls out for fragrance. I see Roly pausing at my row and remember his telling us about the coming of Elijah, how we will each get to ask just one question, and I wonder if mine will be why I was destined to be my father's daughter.

I do not attempt to sort through all of this. Instead, my thoughts return to one of Avivah's recent talks, inspired by the chapter about Jacob our forefather in search of his mother, the very one that ran through my mind on Shavuot eve. After twenty-two years away, Jacob made a vow to return to his father's house in peace and in wholeness. But, as Avivah pointed out, the father's house is really a code word for the mother. When the returning Jacob must bury the faithful Devora along the way, his weeping for her is unrestrained. Avivah believes that Jacob is weeping for closeness unattained with his mother.

As for me, I returned to these shores in time to be with my mother in ways we had never before shared as adults. Unlike Jacob, I was by her side on the cold winter night she died. But did I return to her in peace and in wholeness? Did I return to her in time to salvage all that I lost when I left her — or was it she who left me — so many years before?

All this has come to pass. And yes, I tell Avivah, I have come to some kind of acceptance of my father. But now that I am for the first time communing with a trusted woman mentor, I realize keenly how I now seek a greater understanding of the elusive woman who was my mother. I quietly let Avivah know that, and she nods.

At the meal's end, I lower my eyes and recite the lengthy *birkat ha'mazon* prayer in a low whisper, together with her. I am open to blurring boundaries, to joining my unconscious murmurings and yearnings with hers. I remember how she did not hesitate to give me her blessing, even from that very first written exchange many months ago. A true blessing, she has written, is that of God rejoicing in his work. Her blessings are real and unconditional. They are also procreative, for they hint at future possibilities. They open the door a little wider to my nascent belief that God could be rejoicing in me or, at the least, in my process.

Very soon Avivah will return to Jerusalem. And as for next year, where will we meet, what will we mark, where will our journeys lead, what will we mourn, and what will we be privileged to celebrate? A blessing in her lexicon is a delicious perfume, a sealed vial of myrrh waiting to be diffused for others to imbibe. She awakens a desire I can express for the first time: to come into my own not for the sake of completing my life's journey with fullness, but for the sake of leaving something behind that inspires others. I am not at all clear how I might yet inspire, but I am grateful for the hint, the glimpse, the whiff of possibilities sweetening the springtime air.

A Tourist in Talmud Land

Part Four

From the Fringes

In the springtime, Rabbi Roly's series of lunchtime Talmud classes reconvenes in the corporate sphere. Here on the 38th floor conference room of a midtown skyscraper, suspended between Heaven and Earth, we come together to be close to our *rebbe* and to weave the strands of cryptic narrative into a collective cocoon.

I never expected to revisit the variegated landscape of Talmudic thought, and so far I am keeping my emotional distance, attending class under wraps of several protective layers. For one thing, I am keenly aware of the Women Not Welcome sign that for centuries barred the likes of me from entry to this cloistered men's club. The Talmud is the product of study and debate that took place in the all-male academies of Palestine and Babylonia, schools of learning that flourished for some seven hundred years, from approximately 200 BCE to 500 CE. From these investigations and debates, arising from male-only colloquia of learning, we glean the basis of Jewish custom and law, as well as various frameworks and paradigms for understanding the world we live in. The Talmud is part *halacha*, legal norms, with arguments and prescriptions covering both religious and civil life, and part literature, full of imaginative, almost fanciful anecdotes and commentary under the banner of *aggada*. In its entirety, the Talmud, which here includes the parent body of work known as the Mishna, is a massive body of interpretive riffs on the texts of the Hebrew Bible.

Much is said in both the legal and anecdotal sectors about women. There is a whole section devoted to *nashim*, women — but I have never come across satisfying evidence that any female sensibility on matters concerning them was ever taken into serious account. For this reason I do not expect to experience any personal expansion through Talmudic inquiry. I prefer to think of myself as a cultural anthropologist, here to investigate an earlier civilization in which my own background (not to mention early Christianity and even Islam) happens to be rooted. I see myself as a drop-in/drop-out tourist in Talmud Land, curious but careful not to take any of it to heart.

Still, it is undeniable that for me, as for the others gathered here, Thursday at 12:30 is a highlight of our week. Why do my classmates and I mark these lunch hours as inviolable time-outs from the other concerns of our lives? Every Thursday at noon, too excited to think about lunch, I drop everything and race through midtown crowds to arrive on time and secure a seat not too far down the rectangular table from Rabbi Roly. What is it about this midweek rendezvous that beckons me in closer from the fringe?

"Perversion and Holiness, Stories of the Talmudic Rabbis" — it's a catchy course title, to be sure, and we adore our Rabbi Roly for having the courage to put these quirky tales out there. I am just getting a sense of this man, who is the magnet for so many who flock to the synagogue he leads. He is a Jewish leader with world-class sophistication; he is gentle without being weak; and while he knows his own significance, he utterly avoids off-putting arrogance. He has the capacity to see a broad landscape while focusing on a single detail; he is a private soul, possibly even introverted, but with an uncanny ability to sense the needs of others in his orbit. He is devoted to the well-being of the Jewish people while knowing that their welfare ultimately matters for the sake of the survival of the entire planet. While he himself has soared in some rarefied realms, he is perfectly able to relate to the skeptical on their own terms. He has the kind of spontaneous humor that flashes with empathy for how others see the world. He is a mad soccer fan, and for relaxation he plays the *oud* in an Arab orchestra. He has legions of fans among men who admire his leadership without ever deciphering its secrets; there are women whose only experience of love arises from nearness to this rabbi's never-saccharine warmth. I like the way his purposeful, calm presence transforms a conference room into a sanctuary. I like the way his manicured hands play with the air as though sifting through a kaleidoscope of ideas. I like the sound of his voice, with its soft Spanish accent, his process of free association, and his careful choice of words.

This week we read a bucolic, Rip van Winklesque tale of a prominent rabbi named Honi the Circle-Drawer:

> One day he was journeying on the road and he saw a man planting a carob tree; he asked him, How long does it take [for this tree] to bear fruit? The man replied: Seventy years. He then further asked him: Are you certain that you will live another seventy years? The man replied: I found [grown] carob trees in the world; as my forefathers planted these for me so I too plant these for my children. Honi sat down to have a meal and sleep overcame him. As he slept a rocky formation enclosed upon him which hid him from sight and he continued to sleep for seventy years. When he awoke he saw a man gathering the fruit of the carob tree and he asked him, Are you the man who planted the tree? The man replied: I am his grandson. Thereupon he exclaimed: It is clear that I slept for seventy years. (Ta'anit 23a; all translations are from the Soncino Talmud.)

Looking for something familiar, Honi approaches the study house. He hears the scholars referring to the days of Honi with a certain nostalgia, for it was then, in those good old times, that the wise Honi would settle all disputes. But when Honi lets the scholars know that he is Honi in person and in the flesh, they do not, of course, believe him. Honi finds the obliteration of his personhood so painful that he dies of chagrin a second time — this time, sadly, for good.

Roly speaks of this incident with a great deal of feeling. Clearly he empathizes with Honi's pain at having been wiped out from people's memories a mere seventy years after his prime. Even when I point out that Honi's memory and contributions are still vital after his death, Roly does not seem assuaged. I am touched by this revelation about our charismatic, gentle teacher, whom I am slowly getting to know, a man who gracefully hides any preoccupation with his own legacy.

Finding myself next to Roly in the crowded, high-speed elevator after class, I ask him if it does not suffice that Honi is remembered for his teachings, even if the others do not remember him as an actual person. Roly admits that for him, no, it is not enough. I am surprised, because I do not see the need for validation in the man. Perhaps I am missing the part of him that has fierce attachments or a weakness for grandeur. But this is inevitable, I tell him: We all come, we all go, everything changes. This is the first principle of impermanence so familiar to the legions of Jews such as myself who have detoured into reality-based Buddhist practices. I recognize this as one of the irreconcilable differences between Buddhist and Jewish thought: The Buddhist emphasis on impermanence clashes with the Jewish preoccupation with the past and persistent concern for continuity.

"Surely you can accept that everything changes?"

"No," he confesses, "actually, I can't."

I hear myself say out loud, "Oh, then you are really stuck."

And he softly confesses that around this issue, "stuck" is precisely how he feels. I sense I have pushed a sensitive button, and I don't press it further. I wave goodbye to Roly and deliberately lose myself in the midtown crowds.

If a man forbade himself by vow to have intercourse with his wife, the House of Shammai ruled, she must consent to the deprivation for two weeks. The House of Hillel ruled: only for one week. Students may go away to study the Torah without the permission of their wives for a period of thirty days; labourers only for one week. The times for conjugal duty prescribed in the Torah are: for men of independence, every day; for laborers, twice a week; for ass-drivers, once a week; for camel drivers, once in thirty days; for sailors, once in six months. These are the rulings of Rabbi Eliezer. (Mishnah, Ketubot)

Roly understands this Talmudic discussion to be about the conflict between the attraction of study for its own sake and engagement with the world of people, a tug-of-war between domesticity and devotion to text. It is also about the conflict between a life of abstraction in the realm of ideas and a life of engagement with the social realm. No doubt this is so. Still, I feel there is blatant awareness informing this elaboration of marital duties. I raise my hand to comment. There is an implicit understanding — which surprises me — that going off to study is a convenient escape from the demands of married life. Anyone who has been married for a while knows that between going off and staying put, it is staying home and making it work that is the most challenging of all. What a relief for a guy to get off the hook respectably via a prolonged, scholarly retreat with the boys, where he can cleverly haggle over the fine points of law, rather than painfully excavate his emotional landscape at home.

The room is silent; perhaps I have made everyone a little uncomfortable. My husband sits only a few seats away from me at the table, and E.T. knows the tortuous self-examination to which I refer. He knows the frustration of routine, too, and so, I suspect, does every longtime paired-up person in the room. Still I am giving voice to something that in our circles always remains unsaid. I am coming dangerously close to a personal confession, pushing the self-protection and proprietary envelopes, perhaps implicitly daring all those present to do the same. I catch Roly's eye, and I can see that he welcomes my self-disclosure.

Secretly, I am impressed — deeply, and as never before — by the honesty of the Talmudic rabbis. Here the sages are acquiescing to the unspoken truth that there is, and always has been, a powerful attraction for men to retreat from domestic life and bond with brethren in a separate domain. Within the Talmudic framework, the duel between domestic duties and the appeal of intimate male fraternity is sanitized into a conflict between family life and the call of higher learning. Were the sages not willing to codify behavior, restless and ambivalent men might opt out of marital routines in the name of Jewish learning for unlimited periods of time, thus weakening the all-important fabric of family life.

But there is another focus here. Among the Talmudic sages is a clearly stated concern for the fact that women have sexual desires and that these desires are entitled to fulfillment, even if the marital bed seems dully dutiful compared to the draw of the all-male study hall. I was wrong to conclude that nothing in the Talmud is felt or legislated from a woman's point of view. I say nothing on this matter. Henceforth, however, I will not be holding my cards so close to my chest. Who knows if I won't find support for live issues in the most unexpected of sources?

At about this time, I am tracked down, thanks to the mixed blessings of social networking, by a long-lost boyfriend from my high school years, another dissident from Brooklyn's hermetic world of all-boy *yeshivot*. Back then, he was a wiry, angry young man with smoldering green eyes and a bad-boy swagger, a friend to Hesh and the first to tell me about the right-leaning youth movement known as Betar. At age 15, I found him irresistible in the dark blue shirt and black tie sported by those neo-fascist Zionist Revisionists. He had a quick mind and an acid tongue. A child of Holocaust survivors, he was intent on avenging our national losses. With me, he would let down his guard and read romantic poetry. Although he did not dance, he greatly admired how I did, and often called me his whirling Shulamite. Together we had some kind of pioneering Zionist dream that had something to do with restoring to the Jews their rightful mandate to occupy territory on both banks of the Jordan River.

Since he had been a literary type and had known both Lilah and Hesh back in the day, I decide by way of reintroduction to send him a copy of the recently written "Taiku" prologue to this memoir. With its references to our first departures from Orthodoxy, with its homage to our departed friends, with what had to be the surprising news of my return to New York City as well as to a form of Jewish study, that essay seems as good an introductory overture as any.

He likes the piece well enough, but with the same hostility that was seductive at age 15, he shoots back with a snarky put-down of my misplaced allegiance to the liberal likes of Rabbi Roly. "I find it problematic, but hardly surprising, that Roly — who probably couldn't parse a *sugya* of Gemara on his own if his life depended on it — chooses to entertain a room full of *amei haaretz* (ignoramuses) with a pruriently sensational and greatly atypical piece of shmooze that took place on a slow day in Pumbedita. And, sadly, they think they are actually learning Gemara . . ."

This is just a bit of what he writes in his ex-*yeshiva*-boy jargon. I remember how in the old days, during the weakness-for-tough-guys phase that I share with just about every woman I know, this guy used to beguile me with his vituperative assaults. I no longer find the ersatz bravado attractive. It is shot through with a familiar current of rage that decades ago must have eroticized my own. Whatever is left of my anger, I want no portion of his.

Interesting, too, how my involvement in BJ has made me forget the scorn with which our right-wing brethren routinely dismiss our progressive views. We are wimps because we believe in a two-state solution. We are fools to believe we could ever make a lasting peace in the Middle East. We are in a deluded fog if we forget that as Jews we live in a kill-or-be-killed world, if we neglect the truism that Jews have to concentrate on their own survival far more than attending to any other values or causes, such as overcoming poverty or racism. This self-serving aggression is linked to another form of arrested development, the competitive male brinkmanship thing: My aging old flame stoops to cast adolescent aspersions on Roly, comments I do not consider worthy of even a polite reply. My long-lost friend makes several more attempts to be in touch, but I maintain silence.

Up until now I have felt neutral in my allegiances, always insisting that I am just surveying the BJ scene without counting myself among those loyal to Roly or even to this particular congregation. If the subject arises, and sometimes it does, I strenuously object to inclusion in the (to me transparently foolish) club of Roly's fawning women followers. I am too seasoned to confuse the awakening of the spiritual and the erotic energies, even if I understand their explosive affinity. However I sort all this out, in the moment of this dispiriting Facebook exchange with a former friend, I confess to myself, and for the first time, that I am no longer detached. I dare to admit that I am implicated, invested, involved. I risk a certain level of vulnerability, and with that, I open the door to the possibility of disappointment. I surrender the need to maintain a safe distance and forswear the safety of contrived anonymity. I am my parents' daughter, and I am now a member of an Upper West Side Jewish community; it is as simple and as powerful as all that. I have chosen for myself a teacher and a path. I feel no need to defend my choices to the cynics, be they on the religious right or on the secular left or somewhere in the indefinable wasteland where the formerly Orthodox tend to aimlessly roam.

Heretofore I have been willing to entertain the possibility that Roly might be a kind of guardian spirit to my own fragile and volatile process of spiritual return. It began when out of the blue he asked me to speak on the night of revelation of the paradox that is Ruth. I now sense the possibility of his mentorship gradually blossoming in any number of ways.

I am grateful for what feels to me like Roly's protection as I continue my spiritual exploration. But there is something else at work: I now realize how fiercely I will, if the occasion demands it, protect Roly in turn. I feel grounded in this commitment, and I like the way it makes me straighten my spine.

We read a tale of Rabbi B. Abin, who had a beautiful daughter:

One day he saw a man boring a hole in the fence, just to catch a glimpse of her. He said to the man, "What is the meaning of this?" And the man answered, "If I am not worthy enough to marry her, may I not at least be worthy to catch a glimpse of her?" Thereupon the rabbi exclaimed: "My daughter, you are a source of trouble to mankind; return to the dust so that men may not sin because of you." (Ta'anit 2a)

Roly wants to know what we make of a man such as this rabbi. My answer is brief and to the point. The guy couldn't handle it: He was limited in his emotional capacity, stunted in his growth, unable to integrate a beautiful daughter into his psychic ecosystem. The guy was in overwhelm, and that's how come "he flips out," I say. Roly and many of the others laugh at my not-so-flippant choice of words.

I'm thinking about fathers who flip out while steadying my wavering gaze on the steel girders challenging the sky outside our glass walls. Then I allow my gaze to drift over the urban landscape floating way downtown to the squat tenement rooftops of the Lower East Side, visible only in my mind from our midtown perch. I picture those crammed, narrow streets, overflowing with daily activity. My father told me more than once how the police had to close off all the Lower East Side streets to traffic on the day of his own father's funeral, so great were the throngs who came to honor my grandfather's life and teachings.

Once, my father went to a metal box and took out a yellowing Yiddish newspaper with a front-page photo of the funeral gathering. I sensed that my father did not feel at ease dwelling on the circumstances of his own father's death. As I heard it from his older sister, my Aunt Sophie, the esteemed rabbi suffered a heart attack while riding on the subway next to my father, a painfully shy young man who was forced to helplessly watch his father go from a living pillar of everything that mattered to a mere mortal dying of asphyxiation in the city's underground.

Neither my brother Joseph nor I ever met this grandfather of legend, though his bearded face with sorrowful eyes peered out at us from behind wired spectacles in framed portraits in the rooms of our childhood home. Many of our teachers in the *yeshiva* day schools we attended were brought to a reverential hush when they read out our family name and learned that we were indeed "Ha'rav Reimer's" grandchildren.

At the dawn of the 20th century, my paternal grandfather had a dream of leaving behind the poverty and prejudice of Lithuanian Poland and settling his family in America, a land where he had heard Jews were allowed to study, practice, and worship freely. He came ahead of his wife and six young children, just before the outbreak of World War I. While he suffered cruelly from the complete break in communication imposed by the war, on these shores, Rabbi Yosef Dov Reimer was already a revered teacher and scholar. On the Lower East Side he was a founding educator of the first *yeshiva* for Eastern European immigrant boys. Before they tore down the original Henry Street building of the Rabbi Jacob Joseph School, my father, Rabbi Reimer's youngest, would take my brother and me to see the plaque that was affixed to the facade of the building honoring the memory of our grandfather.

Like the mentor of his spiritual lineage, the Chofetz Chaim, our grandfather was a staunch non-Hasid. His was not an inclusive tradition softened by imaginative tales and soulful melodies; he was a legalist and a crusader, not a mystic. I have never heard reports of him dancing in ecstatic fervor. Rather, he was known for the intricacies and subtleties of his Talmudic discourses. At the age of 13, on the occasion of his bar mitzvah, my brother had to recite our grandfather's most famous *pilpul* (nuanced argument), which he did, word for word, for a full seven minutes, without being offered so much as a clue as to what the recitation was about.

No, my brother Joseph and I never met our grandfather directly, but we nonetheless grew up in his presence. We did not need to meet the man to know that he had little sympathy for slackers. We did not have to know him personally to intuit that his temper was not always sweet or restrained. We were offered full scholarships to all of the New York area day schools because of our *yichus* (family status). Neither one of us could miss the way our teachers drew a sharp breath when they learned of our provenance. There was some unspoken way in which our grandfather's dedication and intensity seemed still to mark the grown men who, from elementary right through high school, stood before us teaching his ways.

Looking back, I don't think my father ever dared carve out a dimension to his identity apart from his role as the youngest and most devoted son of a religious leader. A psychoanalytic perspective would certainly point to that traumatic day on the subway when my father failed to save his father's life. It follows that my father would dedicate the rest of his own troubled life to assuring that at least his father's teachings lived on through him and his children. My coming of age in the late 1960s and '70s was not something my single-minded and unworldly dad had figured into the equation. The mind-dulling drone of Ashkenazi Orthodoxy didn't have a chance against the psychedelic guitar of Jimmy Hendrix. Drugs, sex, and rock and roll ran riot over the preciously cultivated precepts of rabbinical Orthodoxy.

I know whereof I speak when it comes to the subject of fathers of daughters flipping way far out.

The hour-long Talmud class is over, and we are all loath to emerge from this oddly convivial cocoon. Roly offers us a transitional ritual. As is traditional, we rise to recite the *kaddish* prayer in conclusion of the class. The recitation provides a helpful bridge from one state of being to another; the words will shepherd us from our insulated universe to the city streets. When we rise to recite collectively, I close my eyes and welcome a trance-like vision:

I see my father rising majestically to recite the *kiddush*, holding his polished silver wine cup high in sanctification of the Sabbath. It is a Friday night, I am 17, and he knows I am truant from everything he holds dear. The dining room is stuffy, the smell of chicken fat hovering from the hearth. The air around the *shabbat* candles is wavering. My chest is tightening as my father stands. His usually booming voice catches in his throat. I feel a rash of heat. His hand trembles along with the epicenter of the Earth. From the shaken cup a drop of red wine falls to stain the white cloth. Then he forgets the words he has recited every week of his adult life. With these words, the world was created, and without these words, *chas ve'chalila*, Heaven forfend, the whole world could be destroyed. My father has to hold himself up by leaning hard on the table with his free hand while his tears fall in clear crystal droplets. I have never before seen him cry, his outrage dissolved into sorrow. There is a pause, a suspension of time, a moment that lasts forever. Then one salty drop lands in the center of the red wine stain — one drop, this my stain, the mark of his unravel. The communal recitation of the *kaddish* is over; I open my eyes, the scene fades.

On the way out I once again find myself next to Roly in the crowded elevator. Roly speaks flawless French, and we unconsciously slip into that shared language. To my surprise, I tell him that I knew a lot of fathers like the one in the story *(celui qui a flippé)*, that they were all religious, and that some were even prominent rabbis. *Hélas,* I count my own father among them. But perhaps the time has come, I continue to my own surprise, to get over it, to forgive them with the understanding that they just did the best they could at the time.

Roly does not agree. He tells me it is not admissible that religious Jewish men, and especially those in prominent positions of Jewish leadership, be so easily let off the hook. He says this kind of behavior just isn't good enough, it's not going to see us through. We are inching towards the heart of the matter.

These Talmudic sages were men who spent their lives cloistered in masculine sanctuaries of self-referential Jewish learning. Did all this legal wrangling and weaving of cryptic narrative really hone their capacities as human beings? Does Jewish learning give them — or religious guys in B'nei Brak or in Brooklyn today, or us, for that matter — the tools we need to evolve as human beings? Some of the rabbis had terrible character flaws. Did Judaism as a wisdom tradition help these guys out of their ruts? Did it make them more sensitive to others? Did it provide them with a reliable guide to their own souls? Did it make them more present and effective in this world? Are the principles that underlie this tradition those that will help us treat one another with more justice? Does this tradition help us to overcome our own weaknesses and live with an expanded capacity for faith, humility, kindness, truthfulness, and joy? Does it help us respect the environment, see the Divinity in all of Creation, reverse global warming, or take effective action for income equality?

In the spacious marble lobby, people with attaché cases are rushing all around us, eager to take care of pressing business. Roly pauses in recognition of the subject at hand. For him, this is clearly an urgent matter: Is Judaism a body of wisdom that will help us, as individuals and as a society, to evolve? It has to be, he tells me; otherwise, we are all wasting our time. I admire his courage and admit of my doubts. Roly has set the bar high. I fear for him and want to protect him from inevitable disappointment. He does not look daunted, only serious and determined. We both know there will be no lack of opportunities for facing the challenge.

R. Jose the Galiliean was once on a journey when he met Bruriah. "By what road," he asked her, "do we go to Lydda?" "Foolish Galilean," she replied: "Did not the sages say this: Engage not in much talk with women? You should have asked: By which to Lydda?" (Eruvin 53b)

Bruriah is the only woman mentioned several times by name in the Talmud, a woman singled out for her perspicacious mind. Bruriah was a noted female scholar of the turbulent 2nd century, when the devout Jews of Palestine struggled under the might of the brutally repressive Roman Empire.

Bruriah is unique. She is a woman recognized by the rabbinic academy as a scholar of great acumen. It is said that her husband, the prominent Rabbi Meier Ba'al Ha'ness (he was the faithful student of the Acher), particularly turned to her for solutions to ethical dilemmas. It was Rabbi Meier's habit to say to his colleagues, "Rightly did Bruriah tell us . . ." and it seems that in many cases her opinions were adopted.

Bruriah has gone down in Talmudic history as an acerbic harpy. Realizing that she is a lone female in a sea of males, she snipes at the more overtly offensive manifestations of misogyny among the sages.

There is indeed a dictum in the *Pirkei Avot* (Ethics of the Fathers) that warns men not to have any longer a conversation with women than is strictly necessary. Women, they are further advised, are unreliable and lightheaded and will surely drag men down to their own low level. Therefore, when a certain Rabbi Jose meets Bruriah on the road and asks travel directions to Lydda, she chides him for not having restricted himself to the absolute minimum number of words necessary to make his inquiry of a female. A protest and barely veiled ridicule of the prevailing advisory are not so subtly implied.

Together, we read this brief Bruriah vignette in the Talmud class, and then, as he is wont to do, Roly veers off and tells us another tale. This is one about Bruriah that I have never heard, one that I will need to hear a second and a third time to even begin to absorb.

It seems that Bruriah scoffed relentlessly at the boys-club dictum recorded in the Ethics that faults women for lacking gravitas: The word applied to women by the rabbis is "lightheaded" or easily swayed.

Bruriah's refusal to bow to this canard finally exasperates her prominent husband. Troubled by her insubordination, Rabbi Meier vows that some day Bruriah will finally acquiesce to this sexist insult. To this end, the great sage sets up one of his students to sexually seduce his wife. (Yes, you read that right.)

After much resisting, Bruriah finally gives in — not to the truth of the despised dictum, but to the young student's charms. When Bruriah learns that the seduction was a setup by her husband, she takes her own life. In remorse, Rabbi Meier goes off into exile.

I am stunned. We have very little time; we move on to the next story, and all too soon, class is over. Through the recitation of the transitional *kaddish* that ends our study hour, I try to wrap my mind around this monstrous mutant of a tale. How could it be that Rabbi Meier, revered to this day by throngs who gather on the anniversary of his death on the shores of Lake Tiberius to offer up prayers, is the same man who once arranged for a student to court his scholarly wife, instructing the young man to persist until she finally succumbs to his youthful charms?

As it happens, two days later, following *shabbat* services, I find myself at a luncheon seated next to Roly on the occasion of a bar mitzvah celebration. I ask him to clarify: Is that version of Bruriah's seduction and suicide to be found in the Talmud? Where, I wonder aloud, did Roly get that story, and why, I wonder silently, other than for its obvious shock value, did he choose to weave it into our already sullied view of the rabbinic world?

No, no, he eagerly explains, the story is not in the Talmud. This is a story recounted by Rashi, the great medieval commentator. It is a story that explains why it is that Bruriah's esteemed husband, Rabbi Meier, ends up in exile, and how it is that Bruriah's own life story tragically ends. To be sure, Roly adds, there are many who reject Rashi's story, rushing to provide an alternative narrative in explanation of Rabbi Meier's flight out of Palestine. (He had, after all, been a supporter of a disastrously failed rebellion against the Romans, and may well have fled Palestine in fear for his life.)

Think what you will of Rabbi Meier and of womankind's capacity for fidelity; no one I know has ever dismissed the commentator Rashi as a lightweight. Would Rashi introduce a story that puts the esteemed Rabbi Meier in such a compromising light and gives Bruriah a tragic end just because that version of the couple's demise was in circulation?

Roly reminds me that to many readers, Rashi's story is yet another confirmation of the rabbis' prejudice — the very one, we are to be humorlessly reminded, that Bruriah could and should have acknowledged in the first place: Women, no matter how distinguished, are at best fickle and at worst sexually corrupt, sayeth the rabbinic framers of our tradition. But I know that Roly is not telling that story to reinforce sexist prejudices. He has been remarkably forthcoming in exposing the dark side of the most respected of sages. Does he consider it enriching to temper the special esteem in which the legendary Rabbi Meier is held? Or is there some other insight for whose sake Roly takes it upon himself to pass along this seamy tale?

A *doumbek* drum player has joined the small bar-mitzvah orchestra and the familiar Middle Eastern rhythm has me on my feet. I want to explode in a dance, show off my skill at syncopating my hips, isolating my abdomen, undulating my spine. I excuse myself and find a corner on the far side of the dance floor where I dance for my own pleasure, as I often do. This time, my dance is an expression of a certain gratitude not for anything in particular, but for the unfolding of events in a manner that, if I let myself be carried away, seems almost predestined. I end with celebratory spins that make my dress flare out in a joyous sphere.

Next I am joining the raucous clapping and singing that accompanies a childhood country-style dance, wherein we exclaim over the charms of a little bearded goat. I have my hands on someone's shoulders while someone hangs onto mine, as the line sashays and curves around to the silly song. Then, as I haven't done since I must have been 10, we join hands to form the arc of outstretched arms under which, two by two, the ad-hoc couples slide forward and back. In the midst of boisterous exuberance, I begin to see clearly: Like Avivah Zornberg's father, and like Roly himself, I recall that Rashi was the proud parent of daughters, young women whose education he saw to despite a lack of cultural endorsement for these efforts. Clearly, Rashi had no personal interest in sponsoring an insulting view of a singularly learned woman named Bruriah. If he chose to tell this subversive story, it might be to expose stunted development and betrayal in some other quarter.

*All her life, Bruriah rose above what she knew of men, even or es-*pecially the learned sages who populated her world. She knew of their pitiful inability to get comfortable in the presence of a woman who was, at the very least, their equal. She lashed out, but she lived among them; she provoked, but ultimately she accommodated their weakness. She traded skillfully in their currency, managing to push the limits of learning and still land within bounds, mostly on her feet. She scoffed, she upbraided, but she forgave. She outshone, but she tolerated. While she was well aware of the fault lines, she shared their faith in a certain world order. If, indeed, Rashi is right and Bruriah took her own life, she did so out of rage. She cut short her earthly experience because of unbearable disillusionment and the inevitable rage that would engender. Unable to turn that rage against the others, she turned it against herself.

The foundational myth of a traditional Jewish upbringing (and for that matter, just about all traditional upbringings) is that men are more central than women, while women were created by God to be men's servants and helpmates. Men are fashioned in the Divine image while women are derivative, one giant step farther away from God. This is not some outmoded paradigm to which I make nagging reference: The social, religious, and organizational hierarchy of mainstream Jewish institutions is still notoriously, exasperatingly sexist. In traditional families, fathers run our households while mothers make the masculine will manifest in a myriad of appreciated but far more trivial details. Our brothers have the rightful portion of leadership and learning, and only the most exceptional of Bruriah-type daughters may partake in a portion of leftovers.

Withal, there is a subterranean, unspoken counter-knowledge, a heterodox truth alluded to in whispers, hinted at in hushed laughter. It is a knowing that prompts the Not Such a Good Girl to act with integrity; it is a knowing that distinguishes her from the strictly compliant. We daughters live in daily awe of the strength of our mothers, much as we frequently intuit the fragility of our fathers. We understand that the established order has been imposed in order to restore to men a power base they do not come by naturally. In my childhood home, as in many others, the intimation of this reversal of assigned attributes had to go underground. It was far too subversive to be spoken, much less acknowledged or explored. After a while, it bore a tunnel of silence between my mother and me, a no-woman's-land that neither one of us could manage to forge through. Maintaining an illusion has all kinds of hidden costs. Today, my returning to the world of ancient tradition calls for addressing a deceptive imbalance.

And you will love the Lord thy God with all your heart and all your soul and all your might . . . I grew up with that dictate, from the *Sh'ma*. Once upon a time I recited it three times a day. Then I furiously denied it, then left it behind — only I kept coming back to it, again and again. It is a potent directive, an exhortation, a gauntlet thrown, and an enormous enigma. There is no getting away from it any more than we can hide from the pulse of life itself. Yet the dictate, "And you will love," falls oddly on the ears. How can anyone respond with sincerity to such an order? How can true love be commanded? My immediate reaction is defiance — yet there is no escaping this exhortation, which is the erotic energy-charge of the entire cosmos.

And you will love the Lord thy God . . . Some say the word "love" here also means loyalty. Bruriah, most loyal, can you tell me: What if the man you revere with all your heart is unmasked as a pretender to the throne? What if behind the holier-than-thou curtain he is revealed to be a shockingly disloyal partner and a deeply insecure man? We deify. Must we always be at the ready to depose?

. . . *with all your heart and all your soul and all your might.* But what if, in the formative experiences of your coming-of-age, you glimpse that your might is mightier than his, mightier than that of your father/husband/brother/boss? What if, venturing a world-shattering step further, you find that your might is his undoing? I see my father's tear landing in the center of the red wine stain. What can we really know of love? What havoc might we wreak in its name? Might it not be better to steer clear of such absolutes? Yet . . . we are commanded . . .

And you will love . . . the Orthodox wife, mother, daughter is groomed to love something bigger, something better, something stronger and more reliable than herself. All along you suspect and you deny (Bruriah, listen to me), you glimpse, you look away, you grapple and yet you cling tight, you see the chasm and yet you reaffirm the world order. You make yourself small even as your umbrage grows large. You snipe but you do not shoot to kill. Then one day you are stripped naked — *ve'at arom ve'arya* — and there is no covering up all that has been exposed.

The rabbis say that illicit uncovering of genitals is one of the three sins whose avoidance calls for giving up your life. But Bruriah, you did not end your life in expiation for this sin. You ended your life when you were stripped bare and disgraced by those to whom you deferred. Yours is a state of alienation so utter that it will blacken all of our worlds, unless we have the courage to touch you in your shivering nakedness.

Bruriah, here is my confession: I am you, secretly aching to be one-upped in wisdom by the men to whom I occasionally and begrudgingly defer. I am a closet Delilah wielding my shears, secretly wishing my victims would wake up and contain me, and not necessarily with gentleness, before their strength is drained by my cunning, before their authority is unhinged by all that I know.

So then, spirit of Bruriah, you begin to see how commitment to spiritual evolution thrusts us into the vista beyond the patriarchal deception. Ultimately you could find no place for yourself in that no-man's land. And yet, and still, and relentlessly, *you will love* . . . How do we love when the illusion of the All Powerful is shattered? How do we love when the illusion of the All Righteous is smeared? How do we live with everything that we know and all that we are? A secular Jewish poet I admire, Muriel Rukeyser, once said, "If one woman told the truth, the world would split open." Maybe it already has. Who's going to be around now that it's time to pick up the pieces?

> R. Rehumi who was frequenting the school of Raba at Mahuza used to return home on the Eve of every Day of Atonement. On one occasion, he was so attracted by his subject that he forgot to return home. His wife was expecting him every moment, saying, "He is coming soon, he is coming soon." As he did not arrive, she became so depressed that a single tear began to flow from her eyes. Her husband was at that moment sitting on a roof. The roof collapsed under him and he was killed. (Ketubot 62B)

Self-deception: There are times when we see it in others, spotting the flaws in a tightly constructed worldview as seen from the outside, but by definition we are not aware of our own blind spots and misperceptions. Who is not captive to her own way of interpreting events? Who among us does not resort to life-saving denial? Mrs. One Tear, as I have come to call her, is nonetheless an extreme case. Her husband has abandoned her for his studies in the big Babylonian city of Mahuza, granting her a brief, once-a-year return visit on the eve of Yom Kippur. (Note: This is a 24-hour period of fasting and prayer, when sexual relations are forbidden even between lawfully wedded couples.) *And you will love* . . . still, she clings to her belief in his version of marital devotion. Sure enough, there comes a year when he is sufficiently far gone in his selfishness, or love of his studies, or infatuation with his own image in the mind/body of another man, that he fails to make the journey from the academy to his home, even for the Eve of Atonement. Instead — alone or accompanied, we are not told — the absentee husband goes up to the roof of the study house and exults in the heavenly stars. But when a single tear of lucidity falls from his wife's eyes, the roof collapses and he dies. The Talmud seems to be suggesting that in a single crystalline moment of a woman's long-dormant awareness, whole institutions, whole paradigms, may well give way. Even if they give way only in the mind of metaphor, no wonder the troubled rabbis counseled one another against getting overly involved with the daughters of Eve.

I think of my father and his single tear that splattered the wine stain at our Friday-night table. Was it in that moment that he realized I was lost to his way of seeing the world? In a certain sense, he was right. Then again, perhaps he was mistaken. Fast forward (if only we could) into the future unknown and *hineni*, here I am, *venashuva*, and we do return, grappling with ancient world views in a whole new way.

My niece Ziva, my older brother's younger daughter, seems discreetly amused when I tell her I've come to our late lunch after a noontime Talmud class. I jump to the irritating conclusion that she doesn't think we "liberals" are capable of serious study. (Then again, I often imagine hearing allegations, especially in the religion department, that haven't exactly been voiced.)

Ziva's recent conversion to Orthodoxy has taken me by surprise. I never picked up on her inner spiritual seeker. She graduated NYU wearing low-cut tank tops, body-hugging skirts, and platform shoes, and looking proud of her pierced nose and foxy swagger. She was to the left politically, and exuded a hip insider's confidence. One year later, on a return trip from Jerusalem, she is wearing a shapeless, ankle-length frock, sensible shoes, a kerchief tightly wound around her head, and the kind of rimless glasses I recall from a photo of my paternal grandfather, sternly peering at us all from his frame.

What is this all about? Why, after a year away, is she requesting a lunch out with her renegade Aunt Suzi? I've overheard discreet rumors of a disappointing love affair, a subsequent encounter with the missionary Chabad. I sense a quest to replace her mom's radical feminism and dad's liberalism with something more emotionally demanding — or perhaps simply a need to reconnect with ancestral legacies. Neither her parents nor her older sister has offered me further clues.

We settle in at a table at a glatt kosher, ersatz "Japanese" restaurant where the carpets are worn, crumbs are strewn on the table, and techno-fueled klezmer blasts through the speakers. Bearded men rush around with aimless self-importance, and a woman in an ill-fitting wig finally decides to take our lunch order.

Ziva wants to know why her old friends act as if she is no longer the regular girl they once knew. Why is everyone looking at her strangely? I do my best to explain that it is she who has set herself apart, leaving the others to adjust, for better or worse, to her declaration of radical difference. I do have to confess, when she asks, that yes, there is some judgment implied, both in what her choice says about others who have not adopted the same path and, reciprocally, in the others' lack of ease with her unexpected choice. (I remember suffering my own hurt over communal exclusion when, decades ago, it was I who left the fold of my own accord; I decide it might not be all that helpful to bring up that lopsided analogy.) After two hours of conversation, with a burgeoning mound of rejected tuna morsels piled up in a corner of my plate, I'm ready to wrap it up.

"You know, for me, it all summarizes itself in a single sentence."

She wonders what it is but doesn't venture to guess.

"*Ve' ahavta* . . . and you will love." We finish the phrase together in the original Hebrew, as if we were one. She's intrigued and confused, bristling but reflective. So I push the envelope a little.

"You're a woman, a very young and vulnerable and curious woman. As women, we need to choose something to serve as the object of our erotic energy. It seems that for now, you feel best with something eternal, fixed, unified. I understand. This love carries no guilt, no passion, admits of no shame. You're quite sure it won't betray you as long as you play by the rules."

She stares at me, speechless.

"God as the ultimate tough guy," I conclude, "with the heart of gold. It's plenty seductive."

She is provoked but not antagonized. She holds her ground, looking challenged but curious. She's a smart girl and we both know it. This is tricky territory, but it is good when two women can talk.

And I will love . . . I love these young women of the next generation — Raphael's longtime girlfriend, my two nieces, their many friends whom I've met, my own two sons' young women friends, Lilah's three grown daughters, the daughters of other friends. By now, Lilah's first-born, Shira, has become Orthodox, along with her two younger sisters. The once-lithe and carefree roller-blading girl I knew has had a child every year since her marriage to a South African *ba'al t'shuva,* a *bashert,* predestined, whom she discovered thanks to Divine intervention working its way into her life via JDate. Her once-flowing hair is shorn, her skull is encased in a tight kerchief, she's given up vegetarianism to offer up pot roast and chicken fat to a satisfied mate. She no longer smokes marijuana, nor does she listen much to the Grateful Dead. Her once-slender hips have spread wide. I wish her only happiness in her choice, and something tells me she has found her fair share of serenity.

There are young women of the next generation who find comfort in Orthodox tradition, while many of us who were raised in it clash with its insult and exclusion. I have heard Ziva say that tradition insulates her from the indignities of secular culture. I know that communal belonging is balm to Shira's grief over the untimely loss of her mother. These daughters, left rudderless by our lifetime efforts to define our own path, have returned to a male-defined authority system. I want to find a way to tell them that we, their mothers and sisters, their aunts and close friends, are not spiritual deadbeats looking for the easy way out. We did not abandon Orthodoxy to worship at the local mall. We are convinced that God has the capacity to evolve along with our own expanding consciousness. We know that no universal wisdom limits us, as seekers, to second-class, separate-and-unequal status.

I would like to split open and explore the dynamic behind these young women's need for a male-dominated Code of Law. I would like to invite them to consider connecting with the wisdom of women's collective unconscious. What happens to a woman in that oceanic place where she breaks free of imposed sensibility, where she transcends the fear-soaked *gezera* worldview and claims her full stature? Might she dare to trust that she will be guided by some core essence in a province where no male lawmaker has agency? Once a woman is out of the sway of male psycho-spiritual dominion, what is it that grounds and inspires her autonomy?

Homa, Nahmani's widow, came to Raba and asked him, "Grant me my allowance." And he granted her an allowance. "Grant me," she demanded again, "an allowance for wine." "I know," he said to her, "that Nahmani didn't drink wine." "By the life of the Master," she replied, "I swear that he gave me to drink from horns like this." As she was showing it to him, her arm was uncovered and a light shone on the court.

Raba rose, went home and solicited Rabbi Hisda's daughter (his wife). "Who has been today to court?" inquired Rabbi Hisda's daughter. "Homa," he replied. Thereupon she followed her, striking her with the straps of a chest until she chased her out of all Mahuza. "You have," she said to her, "already killed three men and now you come to kill another." (Ketubot, 65a)

I began coming to Rabbi Roly's lunchtime Talmud class with curiosity mitigated by a self-preservation clause. I assured myself that none of this would impinge upon my emotional equilibrium or change my perception of the real world. Then there came insights into marriage, and tales such as this one, which seriously undermine my resolve. Here's how I interpret and expand upon the cryptic tale of Homa, Raba, and Raba's indignant, if nameless, wife:

Mahuza, Babylon, circa 325 C.E. There has been no rain for months in this bustling commercial city. Homa steps lightly, as if the heat and the dust have no hold on her, as if her ears are not assaulted by the din of creaking carts and the cries of hawking merchants. There is always something about Homa that is errant, untamed. No one can ever say which of the many laws safeguarding the modesty of women she transgressed. Imposing limits on such a woman is like banning the frankincense from giving forth fragrance or commanding a tangled vine to grow straight.

The esteemed Raba, presiding over the rabbinical court, has always avoided spending time with her, and has never inquired of his nephew Nahmani about his domestic life. Still, Raba is the great adjudicator and must deal fairly with community funds; he must impose order on chaos; he must resist the haunted realms. He must resist, too, his grief for the tragically felled Nahmani. Rumors aside, who can say what sapped his promising young nephew of his life force? He, Raba, must rise above his emotions; he must remain clear-headed and decide justly in this matter of the widow's allocation.

He grants Homa a standard pension, but she insists that she and Nahmani were in the habit of enjoying wine. For this she requires more funds. When Raba doubts her, Homa raises her drinking goblet high, and the soft folds of linen slide off to reveal her beckoning arm and to uncover the curve of her sun-kissed shoulder. What is more, at that moment, a dazzling light known as the *nahora* floods the courtroom. Though he tries to avert his gaze, through the glow Raba glimpses her dark, incendiary armpit before he rises from his chair.

He rushes home and insists that his wife, Rabbi Hisda's daughter, interrupt her silk inventory. Even if she loses count, he cannot be made to wait another minute. Surprised, delighted, she drinks in his irrepressible desire. But when this blissfully ravished wife comes back to her always-keen senses, she asks him, with something more than idle curiosity, whom he met with before coming home. Because he is honest, because he is naïve, he replies without deception. "Homa." (He does not tell her about the dazzling light.)

Raba's wife wipes the drip of his emission off her thigh. How could she have been so vulnerable in her own terrifying need to be loved by this remote and inaccessible man? How could she have been so defenseless, believing that it was she, wife of Raba, daughter of Hisda, who lured him home, when in truth it was a vixen who turned her husband into a horny goat? It was because of a succubus that he came into her so desperate and undone. A cheap temptress brought forth from the depth of her pious husband such piteous cries as she has never heard. What is she to do with this glimpse into the lonely, unswept corners of a great man's soul?

Homa didn't even have the money for a wedding dress the third time around. It was she, the daughter of Hisda, who endowed that vulgar woman with three full meters of fine silk for her nuptial robes. How did Homa provoke Raba? Was it a fluttering glance, a stray lock of raven hair beckoning from under her headscarf? Or was it a stolen, if deliberate, flash of her shapely ankle, with the straps of her leather sandal snaking a path high up her leg?

Raba's wife squeezes her eyes tight against the intrusion of the vision and feels that she will break apart from shame . . . *with all your heart and all your soul and all your might* . . . Through him, for a fleeting moment, she felt herself lifted up as never before to God. *And you will love* . . . For just one moment she was infused with the purest meaning of those words. Now she is tainted by a dirty and barbaric secret. Homa's sexual wiles have already drained three husbands of their life force. Homa the death-dealer . . . and now her own husband . . . how has that woman dared . . .

And in those days, Raba's good wife was known to be righteous in all of her ways. She could discern who were the truth-tellers and who spoke falsely. It was she, daughter of the wealthy Hisda, who welcomed these hungry students and their grateful wives around her Sabbath table; it was she who ensured the smooth running of the pious community in exile. A woman like Homa was too much for a besotted man in a court of law. The good wife's clouded eyes land on the buckled straps that bind the heavy chest of drawers. She rips the straps off and rushes off under the still-scorching sun. In a cloud of dry dust, reeking of sweat, indifferent to the stares of the merchants and the smirking of the servants, she flogs and curses that she-devil Homa right out of town.

Midtown Manhattan, some sixteen hundred years later, 38th floor. We discuss it all, not without passion. I find myself impatient, impolite almost, with women who insist that poor, defenseless Homa only meant to display her supporting evidence and intended no seduction. To me it is quite clear: In a situation in which we are granted little power, resourceful women will rely on whatever powers of persuasion they do have.

I dare to take the part of the outcast seductress. Then again, how well I understand the slighted feelings of the wife. Once upon a time, I was that siren, luring men away from too narrow an understanding of what it means to take full pleasure in God's world. Now I am a veteran of a thirty-two-year marriage, and I know a thing or two about the incompatibility of passion and trust, how love in captivity scrounges and scrapes for the in-house spark. How, then, might a wife respond with emotional maturity, rather than rage, to the disruptive intrusion of another?

I think of that impious, self-preserving Homa, and I think of the slighted rabbi's wife, and without warning, another more-piercing insight breaks through. It is no secret that a prime ingredient in the recipe for rage is repressed passion. I think of the ripening daughter, and the thwarted nature of my own father's passions, and it makes me wonder if the triangular constellation that pits two women against one another was not the genesis of the never-named alienation that crept in between my mother and me.

Internal dynamite. I had firmly intended to be only a tourist in Talmud Land, but I have lost myself in this drama with soul shards flying all around. I am she and she is I and then comes the other woman making a claim on me as well. That Thursday afternoon, I am not entirely intact as I make my way home.

The memory pops up on the uptown local when the train lurches, and I almost fall, so absorbed am I in thinking about that widow named Homa who bares her arm in the rabbinical court. The more I think of it, the clearer it becomes that this memory is triggered as much by Bruriah's tragic fate as it is by Homa's temerity.

One summer in the Catskills, when my older brother Joseph was about 7 and I wasn't more than 4, I insisted on coming along when he went off into the forest to hang out with the guys. He forbade me to follow, but I cheerfully ignored him. He called me names, and still I kept up with the gang, never losing my trusting gaze. He threatened to hurt me, but never believing that he really would, I ignored him and kept on trailing the boys with an adoring smile. Finally, in desperation, my brother turned around, pulled up my dress, and yanked down my panties for all to see. I burst into tears and ran away, and I could not soon be persuaded to keep company with him again.

Maybe some time in Homa's little-girl past, someone tried to shame her, too. But as she grew older, she came to learn a clever way of transforming shame into power. A wily, seductive woman will not hesitate to trot out her most effective resources when faced with the challenge of survival.

The Jewish sages have never underestimated the explosive power of a woman's animal sexuality, unbridled and unrestrained. It is for this reason that women are ordered to dress modestly, cut off their hair, and suffer banishment to balconies and exclusion from the devotional quorum. When a beautiful woman unveils her arm, she triggers a blinding beam of heavenly light. But then there is the occasional Bruriah, who seems to be mocking all this, or at least diminishing its importance. Bruriah wants entry into the academy for her wit and her smarts, and knows that she more than merits inclusion. But the grown-up little-boy rebbes just can't get comfortable around her. When all else fails, her husband arranges for one of his students to pull down her pants and for everybody else to gasp. It was left to Rashi to make sure that we all were informed as to where the dark shadow falls.

Homa, Bruriah. It is difficult to imagine two more different types. Yet they share a rare mention by name in the Talmud, along with a self-styled anti-*gezera* stance for which, if our sources are to be believed, both paid a hefty price. In truth, they lived countries and centuries apart. Still, there is a whole lot they might have learned from one another: Imagine Bruriah grounding Homa in the cultivation of an able mind; imagine Homa helping Bruriah to transform humiliation into clout.

It is Bruriah's destiny that has me in its grip, and I try to piece together the little that is known about her. One of the outstanding stories, told to praise rather than bury, is the sad tale of the death of her two sons. In 2nd-century Palestine, there was not only the Roman oppressor, there was also the plague. The two sons of Rabbi Meier and Bruriah were taken ill. They both expired on a hot *shabbat* afternoon, possibly before Bruriah's very eyes.

Ever so bravely, she covers the corpses of her children and resolves not to mar the sanctity of the Sabbath with the unspeakable news.

After the *havdala* service, she prepares her husband for the shock by way of a little story with a built-in question. A man has been lent two precious jewels for an unstated but limited period of time. Finally the owner of the jewels comes to reclaim them. What should the man do? Why, naturally, he must give back that which he has on loan, however he has come to treasure it, Rabbi Meier replies. Then the light of understanding slowly dawns in her stricken husband's eyes. Bruriah leads him in the customary benediction: *The Lord has given, the Lord has taken away, let us together bless the true judge.*

It seems to me that Bruriah, until the moment when she allegedly takes her own life, shows supra-human restraint around the cruelest grief. What's more, she is an apologist for the True Judge. She does not shake her fist at *achzar*, the cruel one; she does not cry out against the *gezera*; she does not rail against injustice. She tends to her husband's sorrow rather than argue with God. This was not the case for all of our foremothers.

My favorite counter-example is our foremother Rachel, a younger sister with sexual allure, an aching need to love, and an unquenchable longing for her husband Jacob. Rachel's legacy does not end with her untimely death in childbirth. She is buried on the side of the road outside of Bethlehem, and from that place she watches over her children as they are taken away into exile. At the sight of her progeny's pain, Rachel's spirit cries out and will not be comforted. There is a wonderful midrash, retold by Avivah Zornberg, that takes her outrage a step further:

Rachel takes to arguing, with remarkable eloquence, with God. Why does he cruelly send his children into decades and even centuries of exile for occasionally straying to worship other Gods? Why is He demanding such exclusive devotion? Why is He punishing His chosen people for their disloyalty to Him?

Just think: She, Rachel, a mere woman, had learned in her own short lifetime to do a great deal better than that. Did she not love and long for her husband Jacob with all her soul and all her heart and all her might? Yet did she not come to the understanding that he was not destined to be hers alone? Rachel's older sister Leah was given to Jacob in her stead, a full seven years before her own marriage to him. Despite her jealousy, Rachel went so far as to help Leah avoid humiliation by whispering to her sister some of the secret love words only she, Rachel, and Jacob knew. This way, her older sister would not be rejected offhand from the marital bed, one that Rachel knew was rightly her own. Despite her heartbreak, did she, Rachel, not put the dignity of her sister before her own needs? Did she not wait patiently for her turn? And all her marital life, did she not tolerate the other women in her beloved's arms?

Why does God not share the largesse that forever pumps, despite her suffering, in Rachel's heart? If she, Rachel, a mere mortal woman, could tolerate her rivals, why can't God? And if she, a departed spirit, will not quiet her voice from weeping as long as her children are scattered and scathed, where is evidence of God's compassion? Why is it that God the Almighty has no tolerance and will not withhold punishment for a few instances of divided loyalty?

Rachel will not be comforted; Rachel will not stop crying out; Rachel will challenge this God and hold up her own enlightened example as a repudiation of God's limitations. Rachel our foremother had a more highly evolved understanding than God of what it means to love. So she lifted up her voice and did what she could to help this God — so needy of love and so inexperienced — expand His capacity to give with no expectation of something in return. An early anti-*gezera* activist, she cries out from her roadside grave for the kind of maternal understanding that either in a single moment, or more likely over time, might shift the worldview of God.

"Boys will always be boys, you know."
  "Why don't you clean up your act, Ms. Homa?"
  "How could a woman smart like you, Bruriah, be so foolish?"
  "Why don't you get yourself an education?"
  "A lot of good it did you."
  It all starts late one night. Homa tells Bruriah she should never

have taken it all so much to heart; after all, be they rabbinic sages or not, there is always that fragile male ego. Bruriah feels she has nothing to learn from the uncultivated Homa, even if there are signs that this unschooled woman might have a good mind to go with her irresistible body.

"Bruriah, you were always playing a man's game by a man's rules. No wonder you could never win."

"And you, Homa, smarty pants, what exactly did you win?"

"Staying alive. I've got a real-world survival strategy."

"Even if now and then you are driven out of town."

"Well, I never was a one-town woman."

They have it out for a while, but it does not end with these two. Before I know it, others are joining in.

"How could you have praised the same God who cruelly cut short the lives of your two sons?"

It's the never-to-be-consoled Rachel, calling out from her grave of perpetual non-rest. Bruriah's mouth is open as if to say something, but the realization that this is Rachel, the venerable foremother, silences even the sharpest female wit.

Then a more strident voice pierces the night: "I told them to fix that rotting roof before someone got seriously hurt."

It's the stalwart wife of Raba, calling out to Mrs. One Tear. It was to her husband Raba's academy in Mahuza that One Tear's delinquent husband escaped all those years.

"How many times did I warn them it could collapse!"

After the tragic accident, Mrs. Raba, who was unfailingly diligent in such matters but unable to get a building specialist to come in time, promptly sent her condolences to the bereaved Mrs. One Tear on behalf of Raba and the entire academy. But her letter was returned, marked "addressee unknown." It seems that Mrs. One Tear, who never before left hearth and home, has gone her way, and no one is informed of her whereabouts.

"Hey, honey, you don't have to hide away in shame. Stick with me and I'll show you the ropes."

"Homa? You of all people? You are the last woman . . ."

"Hey, Mrs. Raba, at least I would have set her straight. I could have told her years ago that husband of hers was never coming home."

Mrs. Raba also calls out to One Tear: "Why did you not inquire of me? Why did you wait? Why did you trust? I was the one to turn to in these matters. By now, you might have been mother to many sons."

I see Rachel pressing her bony hand with its emaciated fingers over her ears. She wants to silence Raba's wife. She can't bear the shrillness of her voice. Besides, Rachel strongly objects to the woman's rough treatment of Homa.

"How did you have the nerve to drive another woman out of town? All you had was an imagined rival. Did I, Rachel, not make room? Did I not make space? Accept? Conspire? Tolerate?"

The voices carry on far into the night.

Long after midnight, Homa is beeping Ruth. She has something to say, something that concerns the Moabite stranger woman, forebear of the Messiah: "Hey, did anybody see that? When I raised my arm to show off the goblet, the whole place went dazzling white."

The Talmud says that with the raising of Homa's arm, the entire court was flooded with an otherworldly light. This *nahora*, mysterious light, is a reference to the illumination that heralds the dawn of the messianic age.

"I only meant to dazzle the guy with my arm, and suddenly there's this flood of light."

"I see you're finally cultivating something besides your looks."

"Bruriah, you butt out."

Homa keeps on beeping Ruth. She wants to know why it is that the baring of a woman's shapely arm causes the rabbinic court to be flooded with such a heavenly light. She is asking Ruth — the issue of incest, the bearer of the messianic seed, she who lay down unbidden at a man's feet — what might be the connection between unsanctioned seduction and the long-awaited redemption.

I listen carefully right until the birds begin to sing at dawn, but I cannot hear anything that might be taken for Ruth's reply.

Almost . . . Almost

Part Five

Days of Awe

I'm feeling invaded, uneasy, stirred up, and vaguely defiant. It is conventionally understood that Rosh Hashana, the Jewish New Year, is the anniversary of the creation of the world. But more precisely, Roly points out, it is the anniversary of the sixth day of Creation, the day when according to the Genesis account, we human beings were created. As the annual date comes around, trepidation eclipses frivolity: Each of us is called upon to consider if and how we merit a renewal of our own tentative lease on life into the New Year. What process can we undertake to improve our personal qualification for another round? What can we as individuals contribute to the well-being of the whole? Will we be able to persuade God that we are worthy of living another year? He is known to be a strict judge, but also a compassionate father.

I can't forget the terror that would ravage me as a child at this time of year. We were educated in a rigid, simplified schema of hard-earned reward and well-deserved punishment. Who among us 9-year-olds did not have something to hide? Who among us could claim to have lived up to all the impossibly high standards of our Torah? A sidelong glance from my mother from under her wide-brimmed hat reminded me how I had not kept my explosive temper in check; a stern nod would recall a lie I told about the completion of my homework; a pursed lip pinned me down in an as-yet-unexpiated moment of unwillingness to help with the dishes. I feared that God and his no-nonsense accounting system were not likely to accord me the right to live much past the age of 10. With nowhere else to turn, I would resume swaying and breast-beating with renewed dread and desperate vigor.

Now we gather for the *Slichot* service, a midnight musical overture previewing all the upcoming High Holiday melodies, just before the New Year. On this *Slichot* night, I recall the fervor with which my father would sing the verse pleading with God not to abandon him in his old age, not to desert him in his helpless hour of need. Some time after the midnight service, Dad would sing in a strident cantorial voice into the wee hours of the morning, in an exalted yet supplicant state, as he paced the crowded living room, working up his lather. *Al tashlichenie be'et zikna* — Oh, dear God, do not cast me away when with age, my strength inevitably fails me. My father prayed with all-night ardor to be spared the ultimate indignity of incapacitation.

Yet the musical medley of *Slichot* was not entirely an entreaty against abjection. After the anguish, there came a settling in of an uncustomary peace. I remember the serenity that soothed my troubled dad when, for once, at this time of year, he truly gave it over to God, intoning *haneshama luch,* the soul is Yours, *ve'haguf pe'aluch,* and the body is the work of Your hands . . . *choosa* . . . crooning this time in a limpid voice emptied of its habitual angst, *cho-o-o-o-sa* . . . show mercy to the works of Your hands. And on this occasion — or did I only imagine it? — my father would finally relax with a kind of sweet surrender into a certainty that at the end of his days, a loving God would at last be there to soothe his agitated mind and ingather his radically devoted soul.

This is my first *Slichot* service since childhood. After singing the midnight medley, I find myself walking the few blocks between the synagogue and my home in an oddly straight line, with eyes lowered, placing one foot in front of the other, as if restricting myself to a narrow path. As meditative Jews of all ages and denominations silently float by on the hush of West End Avenue in the wee hours, I walk as though on a tightrope. Does this mean that after a lifetime of wanderings, I am bidden to keep to the straight and narrow at long last?

I am walking with careful delineation in order to keep myself from tumbling over into what appears to me as a bottomless pit. Maybe it's a ravine or an infinitely deep well; maybe it's a chute leading into the mystery at the center of the Earth. All around me, there awaits an uber-gravitational realm exerting its own unearthly pull. This is the bottomless place where you let go of your grip on your ego and your explanations and your plans, the zone where you relinquish your résumé and your masks and allow yourself to free-fall. This is the realm of magnetic force that I have denied for decades, a place where despite your doubts, your resistance, and all your counter-tugs, you surrender your separateness and exhale into the knowledge that, ultimately, it is the spiritual direction of your life that matters above all else.

I am not yet ready to let go. I fear and resist surrender, flat out. I am not ready for a leveling of pride and an annulment of personal narrative. Yet right now, on this walk home, I must exercise great caution. That is why I put one spiked heel in front of a pointy toe, and then another, steadying myself on the punctual clink of the heel against the concrete sidewalk. I take one careful step after another until I can fit my key, as I have done a thousand times before, squarely into the lock of my building's front door. I sigh at the reassuring click as the heavy door yields. I enter the familiar lobby shaking something invisible yet cloying off my back, and clinging to the brick- and-mortar reminders of my life as a rebel.

My struggle comes as no surprise. It is a reckoning well suited to the seasonal rites. My upbringing imprinted me with an indelible template, the knowledge that all our experiences, be they successes or failures, are finite. They come and they go, disappearing, as the holiday prayer says, "like a shattered vessel," and vanishing, in the words of the Hebrew liturgy, as does "a passing breeze." Not for long can I shake the awareness that all of our needs, be they for security, validation or control, simply distract us from the essence. As a Jew, you are invited to spend a tumultuous lifetime sifting through what it is that really does matter, availing yourself of centuries of wisdom literature that came before. Your task is never over and far from self-evident, even if, on the reassuring side, it can and should benefit from certain guidelines.

We know, for example, that as Jews we are this-worldly in our focus, that we are here to take responsibility for ourselves and for others. The ways in which this cultural value will be translated into action is an overarching concern that can keep us busy for a lifetime. The degree to which the course of action we take has an underpinning of faith (as in, for example, derived of Divine revelation) is a question each individual can grapple with all her days.

But I come to this from a very particular place. In an observant Jewish home, a child is cracked wide open, sensitized to an Unseen Realm long before he or she can speak the words. We have a sense of otherworldly gravitas that we never fully shake.

What, then, are we to do? How might we best pass the allotted time between birth and death? The answer is rooted in the cultivation of a particular attitude. The very first prayer a Jewish child learns, one that is recited by all upon waking each morning, tells us that the beginning of wisdom, *reishit chochma*, is the awareness of God. We are programmed to live with recognition of the transcendent. This is why giving up the Orthodox way of life takes such a heavy toll: When you cut ties, you give up a detailed behavioral framework and lose a supportive community. Moreover, you suffer the loss of meaning as you have come to understand it in this world, and forfeit a passport to the World to Come.

The question of how to be an optimal human being is bred in the bones of a religious child, and the answer lies in the details of daily ritual observance as outlined in the Torah. I was raised to understand how every gesture and every choice injected the mundane with a steadying shot of the everlasting. That is the shorthand version of why we Jews have been instructed to wake with a certain prayer on our lips and wash in a ritual way, to bless each act with specified words, to eat and pray and make love according to prescription. All of this minute ritual observance makes us agents of God's will on Earth, keepers of the covenant; it infuses our lives with both practical sanctity and meta-significance.

Why, then, have I turned my back on those ritual forms? Why have I not embraced a well-laid-out path to personal and collective meaning? What is there inside me that has, ever since I assumed selfhood, been animated by the right of refusal of this pre-packaged how-to manual for living the good life? More urgently, what is happening to me and to my precious resistance right now? Am I about to lose my grip on my hard-won autonomy? Am I about to lose my footing and tumble into the prescribed (if contrived) world of my rabbinical ancestors?

Safe now in the shadows of my eighth-floor bedroom, awake like my dad into all hours of the *Slichot* night, I dreamily look out on the lights of a boat drifting up the Hudson. I take a deep breath and anchor myself in my comforting interior. I need to keep my balance on this very narrow ledge. If I pull back and tighten my grip, there will be less risk of teetering over the edge. My life will go on as before. I will be loyal to my own skeptical defiance in defense of self-determination. I will not cast doubt on the value of the rupture that cost me so dear.

But if I teeter, if I plunge, if I exhale into this chasm of infinity, then my religious life, my attendance at BJ, my engagement with text, my social action duties, all these are no longer just another entry in my busy Google calendar. My synagogue affiliation would then shift from its current status as just one more commitment among the many activities that fill my agenda as a self-styled New Yorker to occupy a much larger place. It would swell into a priority over competing engagements; uncontained, it might very well become the very ground of my being. I have always objected to, even mocked, how the Jewish Question intrudes on every other concern for the affiliated faithful. It looms ubiquitous, colonizing the awareness by which all other awareness is nuanced. If I were finally to adopt this framework, would Judaism then become my organizing principle, the guiding light and legacy of my life? I am not comfortable with that scenario. It represents too radical a shift. But why am I holding back? What would it mean if I were to give up the struggle to individuate and simply concede the oversized space this whole Jewish Question occupies in my life?

One danger of such a shift is that it might oblige me to be more of a practicing Jew — to attend 7:30 morning *minyan* every weekday, to avoid non-kosher restaurants, light candles on time, and never plan any travel on *shabbat*, to name but a few of the many halachic obligations I am reluctant to take on. Perhaps if I contemplated this shift coming from a different upbringing, I would not feel threatened as I do by a tightening of the halachic noose. But whenever I drop my guard around the Jewish Question, I feel its rabbinic legalisms gripping in a stranglehold around my stubbornly defiant neck.

I am so caught up in the approach/avoidance of this internal dialogue that I fear I will not sleep this night. Can agitation on a particular night of the year have been transferred from my father to me? That question only adds to my disquiet. This voice inside keeps asking me where I really stand. Do I now finally want in? But how can I be included while still resisting the demands and discipline that are part of the deal? The progressive movement likes to make Jewish life sweet and satisfying; they don't like to ask folks to move too far out of their comfort zone. But I know better than to think I can so easily have it both ways. When Judaism as an ancient tradition moves front and center, there are concessions in lifestyle that ought to be made, and these have gone against my grain ever since I was a teenager. At BJ, I've never heard a discussion of the actual laws of keeping kosher or the Sabbath. Too much of that sort of thing would surely alienate some of BJ's constituents. But lax organizational policy does not make it any easier for me to resolve the issue for myself.

*I find the beginnings of a reassuring response in the writing of a non-*Jewish theologian. There is a realm of conscious awareness that the theologian Paul Tillich calls "the ultimate concern." This ultimacy is not about acquiescing to specific beliefs, nor is it a pledge of allegiance to any particular doctrine to the exclusion of all others. It is not a declaration of certainty. It is, rather, an admission of a certain perspective. As I understand it, Tillich's ultimate concern is the stake in the ground around which we prioritize all the rest. It is the spiritual maypole around which we ingather all the conflicting dynamics of an always-questioning faith. It is an acknowledgment of a concern that we allow to be ultimate.

I have returned to my native land at a time when all sorts of serious-minded, sophisticated people are coming together to ask questions about ultimate concerns. They, we, I are questioning the role of God in our lives, the degree of our allegiance to the past, and how, if at all, the precepts and ritual forms that have come down to us might be effective tools for optimal personal development and responsible world citizenship. It is as if we have all met in the middle of a late summer's night to inaugurate an endless treasure hunt. Often, we will be groping for clues in the dark. Other times, we will stumble upon hints and signposts in the light of day. I am comfortable with joining the search party, delighted with the growing number of women leaders, all the while knowing full well that I will never find a definitive answer to the Great Enigma, and accepting that, at best, some of us will leave a marker or two along the way.

Tillich offers this personal and collective undertaking the lucidity of his language: *An act in which courage accepts risk belongs to the dynamics of faith. This is no restful, affirmative confidence. It is, rather . . . a courageous affirmation of self in the state of ultimate concern.*

This, I realize, is the beckoning, the gravitational pull pursuing me in the middle of this sacred night. It is a call to simply accept myself as a person in dynamic relationship with ultimate concerns. I do not need to renounce my devotion to personal freedom in order to embrace this quest. I do not need to neatly tie up my relationship with legally prescribed Judaism. I do not need to definitively reframe my feelings about God. I need only to remain in relationship with the questions and feel increasing acceptance of their critical role in my life. I need to feel safe when according them whatever space and centrality they would claim. Tillich wisely counsels, *Accept it or deny it, approach or avoid it . . . Our ultimate concern can destroy us, as it can heal us, but we can never be without it.*

Before finally settling down to sleep in the pre-dawn of *Slichot* night, I come to terms with what I know and all that I feel. I can run, I can hide, I can dissemble, I can cross an ocean, I can change my name and don a dazzling assembly of masks; I can resent a God who made me feel transgressive and bemoan a father who never accepted my anti-*gezera* flair. I can even acknowledge the ways my father and I are alike in our capacity for agitation. I can wiggle my way out of a commitment to *halacha* and laugh a little at the outsized self obsession of our tribe. But the truth in evidence is, just as Tillich wisely observes, I will for all my life be grappling with these questions, and they will inform my life in whichever way I choose to live it. As a 21st-century Jew, I can't be without my ultimate concern, nor would I want to be, never, not ever again.

The New Year holiday comes early this year; not two weeks have passed since Labor Day. As it happens, that first Monday in September was for me an unforgettable afternoon, one I have come to refer to as my personal Day of Dread. My response to the *Akeda,* the Binding of Isaac, which we read at holiday time, is colored by the experiences of that day.

Over Labor Day weekend, my younger son, Jonathan, who is 24, is away at the beach with friends. He has promised to be home early on Monday morning, but by noon he has not called or answered any of my phone messages. My mind spins off into a nightmare scenario: He is at a beach known for its riptides, he always calls, every summer someone drowns on this beach, he might not have been cautious, why has he not made contact, there is no other plausible reason. In an instant I slip from an anxious parental snit into an entirely altered state. I am transfixed in tragedy, possessed by a scenario in which I am the mother undergoing the ultimate, unbearable sacrifice.

When, forty minutes later, my son does call, expressing astonishment at my degree of alarm, I snap back to the present moment. I am utterly drained yet eerily, profoundly calm. Out there in "the real world," nothing remarkable has actually happened. Yet I have glimpsed something that has left me both shattered and oddly affirmed. I am emotionally liberated, spiritually open. I can't help but wonder why this is so. The Day of Dread has brought me about as close as I've ever come to personal epiphany.

If pressed to explain, I would say that I viscerally understood something inescapable, without any psychic barriers, and for the very first time. So much of our psychic energy is spent in denial of the ultimate realities: We love and we lose, we live and we die, but most days we do anything we can to dull awareness of these enormities. Yet in my agony on that Day of Dread, I had a tiny glimpse of what it would mean to surrender the struggle. There is a state in which, even for the briefest moment, we brush against an ultimate reality and we sense what it would be like for the ego to desist in its denial of what is.

My thoughts drift to the story of the *Akeda*, a disturbing drama that we encounter during the High Holidays. The story of the near loss of a son at God's almost whimsical command, it is considered to be the central text in the formation of our spiritual consciousness. Volumes have been written about it, and I have little to add to that literature. But now I understand it from a visceral, even if conjectured, psychic experience of my own. Like Abraham, I have lived through a scenario composed of inner fears about losing that which is most precious. Abraham is awakened from his nightmare by the voice of an angel; the ringing of the phone brought me back from mine. Yet both Abraham and I were traumatized into a transcendent moment, a moment that is pivotal in the formation of each of our spiritual consciousnesses. The conclusion, assuming there must be one, might be ultimate faith or ultimate despair; the choice between the two absolutes comes down to an arbitrary mapping of meaning.

We learn in chapter 23 of Genesis, the one that immediately follows the *Akeda*, that Isaac's mother, Sarah, dies soon after the near-sacrifice of her son. Rashi explains that Sarah could not survive the shock and disorientation resulting from her husband's acting out of Isaac's near-death. As is often the case with Rashi, the commentator gives us the heartbeat of a flesh-and-blood woman confronted with the real world when he points out the proximity of the two events: "as a result of the tidings that her son had been fated for slaughter," he says, "and had been all-but-slaughtered, her soul flew away and she died." Sarah is not led to believe that her son has actually died, only that he came exceedingly close. What, exactly, is the shock that causes Sarah's soul to fly out of this world?

In her essay, "Cries and Whispers: The Death of Sarah," Avivah

Zornberg explains that, like most mothers, Sarah is fiercely dedicated to protecting her son from even remote possibilities of harm. She is a mother who, like many of us, seeks to "childproof" the world to secure her son's welfare. She operates under a familiar maternal illusion that she can keep her child safe, if only she takes care of every contingency. When Sarah receives the news of what very nearly was the outcome of Abraham's early-morning outing to the mountaintop, her confidence in maternal caretaking is shattered. Isaac has not died, but had things gone just a little differently, he certainly could have. In her essay, Zornberg speaks of Sarah's "vertigo," her complete "loss of orientation," as "a common reaction to a situation in which one is almost . . . almost."

Sarah is forced to move out of her carefully constructed world of certainty into an untenable place where life is lived on the edge of a blade. Zornberg tells us that Sarah is invaded by "a sense of radical doubt," the existential vertigo "of not being able to preserve one's being. . . . Not being able, from one minute to the next, to live longer than is destined." Zornberg goes on to say that Sarah "dies of this radical angst." Perhaps because of her inflexible nature, perhaps due to her advanced age, "she didn't manage to come through."

I am now past 55, my husband approaches his 70th birthday, my grown sons are out and about in an unpredictable world. The lust for safety is fueled by the ferocity of love; the ego hates to surrender the struggle for certainty. On the Day of Dread I knew I had the same choice as Sarah: I would "come through" by expanding my capacity to be with the fear and the trembling, or, in every meaningful sense, I would die to my own radical truth.

*You might call it a sociological conundrum: Congregation B'nai Jesh-*urun has hundreds of educated people coming of their own free will to a prayer service every Friday night without the big assumption that they are worshipping a transcendent, superhuman God. No one is insisting that we acknowledge the Torah as the word of this God (though it's fine if we do) or that we pledge allegiance to its revelation at Sinai, or that we bind ourselves in observance of every one of the laws. No one in post-Holocaust culture is promoting the idea of God as miracle worker or lifesaver, no one suggests that the Almighty is a reliable respondent in our hour of need. We all know too well that very bad things do happen to perfectly good people. In short, no one here is peddling salvation or proffering relief from a sea of troubles. We are sophisticated; we know that even the most sincerely offered prayers, more often than not, go unanswered.

I have never taken a poll, but Roly tells us that others have and found that among all the major faiths, Jews and Buddhists score the lowest when it comes to certainty about God or any version of ultimate truth. In some ways, this doctrine-free philosophical ambience is thoroughly liberating, but it does leave me to wonder what it is that draws all these well-educated people — many of them heretofore religiously unaffiliated, some of them not Jewish by birth — to BJ for spiritual renewal week after week. What inspires them not only to sing and dance and clap with fervor, but also to donate money and devote many hours to social activism in the local community and in the larger world?

One of the rabbis, Marcelo Bronstein, was asked these questions by some social scientists eager to study the BJ phenomenon. He explained that rather than preach doctrine, BJ purposefully creates an environment for the "exploration and cultivation of the interior self." Here, "touching God" means "touching the essence of life," allowing each person to feel optimally alive. The idea is first to feel better, clearer, and more connected to what may be a lost part of the self. The love (like the holiness) we are seeking in God is a love (or a holiness) we must unlock within our own hearts. The BJ experience is profoundly reorienting. It offers sanctuary from the maddening pace of the world, and in this sacred space, music, prayer, and contemplation connect each of us to an inner core. This spiritual expansion yields a newly sensitized appreciation of our own humanity, and this gives us the courage to act on behalf of others in the larger world.

BJ members are activists for social justice in all sorts of ways: We have successfully lobbied, together with the Church of St. Paul and St. Andrew, for health benefits for local restaurant workers; we maintain a nightly homeless shelter that is staffed by volunteers; we march for marriage equality and we speak up for Palestinian rights to self-determination (sometimes with internal dissension). Prayer that depends wholly on the intervention of an external, superhuman entity seems a little beside the point in this activist hub. Art Green's focus on God as the "actionable evolutionary impulse" within each of us seems far more relevant.

Still, we are left with a certain, shall we say, existential gap. If, as Avivah Zornberg says and too many of us have experienced, God is *achzar* (cruel, estranged) or, at best, unreliable or, irresistibly, at His best when not playing God, to what or whom do I turn in my hour of fear and dread and doubt? How do we help ourselves when facing dark uncertainty? How do we survive the almost-almost-angst that cost foremother Sarah her life?

Jonathan has been staying with us for the past several weeks. It is a few weeks after Yom Kippur, and I have come to cherish our early-morning hour of together-time. We talk about our plans for the day, offer encouragement or a new perspective, weave in something about the day's news or something we have recently read, watchfully prepare some fresh farm eggs (lest they boil for more than a minute), and give one another a quick kiss goodbye.

This particular morning in early October, instead of heading downtown to his job in the numismatics museum, Jonat is catching a noon plane to Dubai with a connection to Dhaka, Bangladesh. He will be away for five months to teach a course he has created called "The History of Ideas" in a liberal-arts university, the only course of its kind in the country. He has also organized his students as volunteers to teach literacy to little girls who labor long days in nearby garment factories.

This is his third trip there, and I can never totally get used to the wrenching distance. I function in multiple dimensions on that departure dawn. At a loss, I keep wrapping up food in little snack bags — here a bag of almonds, there a few slices of cheese, throwing in a banana, reminding myself that liquids will not be allowed with him on board. Jonat alternates between gently saying no thanks and accepting my offering, clearly more for my sake than for his. I putter around my kitchen, assuming overlapping identities: I am in Jewish-mother default mode, I am shaking my head at what I'm like in Jewish-mother default mode. I am, of course, my own mother, whose habit it always was to arm us with provisions even if we were only taking the subway to a friend's house for the afternoon. I am also Jonathan, agreeing to the irrelevance of maternal solicitude when a young man is responding to the call of the wild.

In the days following his departure, I'm into sublimation and denial. In New York City, it's easy to just keep moving. The questions that haunted me throughout the High Holiday season have subsided somewhat, though very possibly they underpin other concerns that loom large. I need to make up for fifteen months of business plans that now, due to the sharp economic downturn, are not going to materialize. I take Middle Eastern dance classes, and my passion for this ancient, by-women, for-women dance form brings me closer to the biblical Miriam, who may well have led her coterie of celebratory women in similar style when they crossed the Red Sea. I attend BJ Friday nights and Saturday mornings, too, always coming away with a hit of inspiration. I keep a journal and continue my signature brand of coaching, which integrates breathing with essential-oil blends as a means of anchoring desired states. I post once or twice a week to my "From the Twisted Fringe" blog, and feel gratified by its slow but steadily growing readership. I begin covering the arts and women's issues in *Jewish Currents* and *The Jewish Week*. There is a new book I am outlining: It starts with God's proclivity for fragrance and goes on to say that scents can play a role in personal evolution as well. I am also taking notes for a book on women in the *aggada*.

The approach/avoidance dialectic that is my loving marriage of thirty years occupies center stage of my emotional life. Then there is my constant seeking of equilibrium in my relationship with Raphael: We still swing from complicity to conflagration with hopeless unpredictability. Sometimes I meet him downtown, where he plays percussion in late-night Village clubs and restaurants, sitting in on sets led by master Cuban, Indian, and West African percussionists. Usually we are joined by his ladylove, Jodi, a young dancer with whom I have come to bond. Sometimes it all seems too good to be true: Together they are meeting their modest Brooklyn rent; she is beautiful, energetic, and adoring; they support one another's artistic ambitions; she is Jewish, a close friend of my older niece; her grandparents hail from a Polish town as do we; she has strong family feeling.

But I know that all is not as well at it seems. There are the persistent irritations: rats scurrying in the hallway when they come home late at night, vagrants who piss on her bicycle. Raphael is playing lots of Westchester weddings but not really making ends meet. They are both being worn down by the grind. Her wealthy parents are backing them financially, and Raphie doesn't like the way that chips away at his manhood. He hints that he is not ready to settle down; he alludes to a need for sexual adventure.

I observe myself clinging to a hopeful outcome, one that will absolve me of all my own neglect of tradition when raising my boys. I deny what I don't want to hear, convincing myself it will all work out. I often go for long, exploratory walks alone at nightfall in the city I love: Walks, like life, are best enjoyed as journeys without fixed goals. Yet I have a cherished goal, or better yet, an ardent wish for the future. I cling to it even as I know it is risky to depend on someone else, much less a grown child, for satisfying closure.

*I sit and stare, unable to move, at the e-mail from Jonathan in far-*away Bangladesh:

Dear Family,

SO I'm sitting on my desk watching my students do their tests. Everything is going quite peacefully, I'm doing some conscious breathing while watching over my students.

All of a sudden there is a loud, thunderous, BOOM!!

Out of the corner of my eye I see special police units running down the main avenue and the usually busy street eerily clear of traffic.

Then machine gun fire starts going off below in the street. Some section of the border guards took over a building one block down the street from where my university is and an as yet undetermined number of people have been killed.

Bangladesh is a lot farther away than the local beach, and machine-gun fire is deadlier than whipped-up surf. If you are a mother, or a dad, or if there is anyone out there in the wide world whom you wish would come closer to home, you know that emotional elasticity and cockeyed optimism are the sine qua non resources of psychic survival.

Then the theater begins. Army trucks arrive and soldiers are running along the sides of the buildings, big clusters of them congregate behind the block corners on the main avenue.

Everyone in the surrounding buildings is looking at the windows, poking their head out of iron curtains of shops and loitering about, hiding any time a shot is fired and slowly coming out again.

Something in me is confused. Is he telling me something that is real? Or is he, as he sometimes does, sending me an excerpt of some fictional account?

I do not really know what to do. My students are here, after all, what kind of example do I give if I run out panic-stricken?

Finally, once my students are escorted out, I go down through the garage where the iron curtain is open to about ten inches above the ground and a bunch of people are yelling at each other. I meet a student of mine, who offers to escort me.

We open the iron curtain slightly higher and run out to safety. I look up and see scores of soldiers in the side street and more pouring in. Like ants they're all over the place coming in from back alleys with plainclothes higher-ranked people shouting orders at them. At this point, I hop on a rickshaw and thank my student. And I am in dream with adrenaline pumping.

Long story short, I make it home safely, through a circuitous route.

Was it for the sake of summoning the necessary inner strength for just such a situation that, not so long ago, my unconscious dragged me through the kind of binding/unbinding imagined threat that ended foremother Sarah's life? Did I need to live through the fully imagined Day of Dread version in order to have fortitude for another far-closer call? By the time I am able to read the e-mail through, E.T. has Jonat on the phone. I hear him saying reassuring things in French, using a calm yet robust voice: *Good thing you are home safe, it will take a little while to unwind, so glad you kept your cool . . .*

There is a part of me, like foremothers Sarah and Rachel, that is refusing to be comforted. One hundred and forty-seven people were killed that late morning down the street from his university in Dhaka, many of the victims ranking army officers, and about twenty passersby caught in the crossfire. Where is it written that we mothers have to develop the inner capacity to imagine our children crawling through raining bullets or stepping over fallen bodies or being bound, for that matter, on any manner of sacrificial altar? I think of all my counterparts in the State of Israel. We are helpless, bereft of all charms or rituals, when our children inevitably go off to earn their badges of courage through the military or an initiation ordeal.

It's a cold but sunny and brisk autumn day. I speak briefly with Jonat, who sounds unconvincingly brave, and I wonder if and when he will experience a meltdown. Then I bundle up and go off for a walk along the Hudson River. When I get down past the boat basin, I find myself in a serious exchange with my mom. I arrive at the promontory on 72nd Street, which overlooks a wide expanse of river. This was the spot where I would help Mom out of the wheelchair so she could look over the low, stone wall and take in the scene, along with the iodized marine air. She is with me on that ground this morning as I lean over the wall, trying to catch my breath in the gusty wind.

Mamele, she calls to me in a tender yet reproachful tone. She wants to know why I let my youngest son out of my sight, how I let him go so far away to an impoverished and hostile place where, far from defending some Jewish legacy, he cannot safely reveal himself as a member of our tribe. *Mamele,* she says, *how could you?*

Sarah: *Men... always playing fast and loose with life and death.*

Avivah: *While we are elsewhere . . . truly elsewhere, they . . .*

Sarah: *To Him, to them, it's an endless game of one-upmanship.*

Avivah: *While we keep our ear close to the murmuring deep.*

Sarah: *They cannot see His face, so they joust with the ultimate . . .*

Avivah: *But we can work from the hidden sphere.*

Sarah: *Hide and seek, seek and hide.*

Avivah: *Go deeper, come from a deeper place.*

Sarah: *I got so tired of this game.*

Avivah: *Life is always lived on the razor's edge.*

Rukeyser the Poet: *If one woman told the truth, the world would split open.*

Rachel: *And so it already has, a million times over.*

Mamele, my mother says, *how could you let him go?*

I have no answer for her, but I have an inkling that underneath the maternal fretting, my mother does understand. Back in Bangladesh for the third time, Jonathan is now spearheading a project to bring bio-gas to a remote tea plantation. Like my mother and my father, he is also a teacher, bringing new ideas to his older students, inspiring them to teach impoverished little girls how to read. While there, he never mentions his Jewish identity. Yet without anyone spelling out the mandate, he is doing the work that hastens redemption.

In the days and weeks following the Dhaka shoot-out, I find myself reciting prayers of gratitude. I resort to a blessing known as *Hagomel,* a special expression of thanks invoked when one's self or a dear one is saved from danger. I think of Sarah and Rachel and my own mother, and all the *mameles* in the world.

These days, when I enter the synagogue on Sabbath or midweek,

I warm to the greetings of others. I begin to bond more deeply with a gallery of women friends whom I have gradually come to know and trust. I became friendly with some in a study group we formed that reads Zornberg together. I know others from volunteering at the homeless shelter and still others from a sub-group or *chevruta* of Roly's lunchtime class that focuses on Talmudic *aggada* dealing with women. Some have become readers of my blog and invigorating co-travelers on the spiritual exploration path. Others were there for me when my mother died and remained with me as we offered comfort to other mourners. Still others remember me from my New Moon presentation about women and visibility, and then there are those who like to exchange ideas about the biblical Ruth. Some of the women I befriend have *yeshiva* backgrounds, as I do, and are returning after a long time away; others are discovering Judaism for the first time as adults; still others are Jews by choice. We all struggle to accommodate the insight that cost foremother Sarah her life. There is no insurance policy, no reliable savior, and it all takes place on the razor's edge.

There is a truth I am claiming for my own: The only balm is in an ingathering of sister spirits. This is not about the esoteric; it is about mutual support, about community as a supportive environment that overrides theological preoccupations. Together we can offer one another the capacity to be fully present. Certainty about the ultimate truth of our tradition fades in importance. What matters most is *hineni*, "Here I am," a shared willingness to be present in community.

I repeat my blessing and let it penetrate into the depths of me, to the same wildly vulnerable zone I glimpsed on my Day of Dread. This is a moment of intense communion with all the *mameles* of history, our moment of birthing the special brand of spiritual strength that is conceived from complete recognition of our fragility. Ours is a cocoon of safety in the midst of violent vulnerability. The coming together of women to support one another — within and without the company of men — is a powerful spiritual act in a world where every minute is a case of almost . . . almost. This is the sanctity of our prayer.

It doesn't matter whom else we might be addressing.

And Then She Will Be Whole

It happens in the very way I had so much hoped it would not: Raphael sits down with me at the dining room table to unveil a decision with which he has been wrestling for a long time. He is leaving New York City. It has something to do with its daily grind, alternate-side parking, and the high price of bread. He is striking out for the desert, where he has been informed by a mysterious source that new opportunity blooms.

I let that much sink in. He is telling me, as gently as he can, that he is going west to, of all places, Las Vegas. There is much work in the entertainment industry there, he explains, and housing is dirt cheap. It is warm all year (when I raise my eyebrows, he reminds me how he hates the cold). He is sure to get a steady, well-paid gig as a percussionist; he is sure his house will have a driveway and he won't have to circle for hours, late at night, trying to park.

I stare at him. I never figured him for the type of guy who would drastically change his life for a parking spot of his own. But I know there has to be something more than that influencing his decision. He is chunking it down, trying to be considerate, warming up my shock absorbers by breaking his momentous news to me in small jolts.He goes on for a while about how soul-deadening it is to play "Feelings" over and over again for Westchester weddings, how disheartening it is to hustle all month just to pay the rent on a tiny apartment in Williamsburg (not the trendy part) where the Orthodox Jewish landlord never gives enough heat and vagrants piss in the hallways. He repeats how hard it is to park when he gets home after those terrible weddings, and how, even when he finally manages to do so, there is no guarantee he won't find his car broken into the next morning. Okay, okay, I get it already. The prelude is over; I am bracing myself for what surely comes next.

Then he lets me know in no uncertain terms: He is not only leaving a life where he is just scraping by. Just as I suspected, this has to do with love — or lack of it on his part. After four years, he is leaving a relationship that is simply not satisfying, even if he knows he may never find such a dearly devoted companion again. He is just not that into devotion, even if he recognizes that these days I am. He wants some sparks. He's into the transgressive. (Could that be congenital?) So — deep breath needed here by both mother and son — he is striking out for Vegas and ending his four-year liaison with Jodi, who is now his fiancée. (They have just became engaged, though no wedding date has been set.) He rushes to add, lest he never find the courage to do so again, that he is involved with another woman, someone very different, someone outside, shall we say, our usual circle of friends.

Raphael is, in my stunned understanding, being lured away to the City of Sin (from Paris to New York City to Vegas — I mean, who does that?) under the spell of some irresistible siren who will not be making him a big pot of nourishing veggie soup while he is off looking for fame and fortune late nights on The Strip. She is, I am being informed by slow-drip method, not of our religion and not of our race. She is lithe and leggy and ridiculously lovely and really it is of no consequence whatsoever to him, not at least in this enthralling moment, if she is not of our tribe.

Poor, foolish, pathetic me. I have taken Jodi deep into my heart, adopting her as a surrogate daughter, projecting onto her all sorts of fantasies about expiation and closure. She and I don't talk about meta-meaning or the big picture much, but she finds in me the understanding, admiring, upbeat mom she is looking for, while to me she is, of course, the daughter I never had. I've been having a wonderful time with our mother-daughter dynamic: We take yoga and belly dance classes together, we create essential-oil blends, we massage sore muscles and exchange books and carouse with one another's friends. She is teaching me to cook vegan, and I share insights from life coaching and hypnotherapy. I give her favorites from my younger-days Parisian wardrobe, and offer tips about style. Yes, indeed, I have cautioned myself over and over again that it is not *my* love for her that counts, but I have never been one to prudently ration emotional satisfaction for fear of later consequences. I was quite simply in denial, never wanting to face the reality that Raphael's attachment to her had a lot to do with pleasing me, while generating little sustainable energy of its own.

Son *(presenting his bottom line)*: I have had enough of trying to live my life in order to make you happy.

Mom *(stun-gunned)*: So this showgirl has convinced you to set off on a journey with no way home?

Son: Just think how your parents must have felt when you told them you were going off to live in Paris.

Lech lecha . . . now go forth. Just this same week, I attended a class with a rabbi named Jan Uhrbach who spoke of this leave-taking as one of the central tensions within Judaism. We know that in order to remain vital, each new generation has to go off, break with the past, and discover new versions of old truths for itself. We must innovate, take a risk, or we will remain forever frozen in *gezera* mentality. But at the same time, we Jews are thoroughly attached to the continuity of our tradition. That is why the sages have to go to some length to explain that forefather Abram, even when heeding the Divine call to leave everything behind, was still not cavalier about cutting ties with his own father. Otherwise, in this portrait of the patriarch as a youngish man, the Bible just might set the wrong precedent. If, even at the behest of God, Abram just took off, leaving behind his aging dad, he would be an overly radical role model.

Jews want their children to go forth and shine. We also want to keep them close by. That's the tension we struggle with in every generation. Whether or not we honored our Jewish legacy in our own youths — and like me, many of us did not — we still want our children to be links in an unbroken chain.

I'm starting to cry, and my sobs are growing less controllable, even though I know this is far from the best parental response. I am not proud. I am not self-righteous. I am defeated. Something inside is pitilessly unraveling. I am crying now for absolutely everything — for all that time I spent far away, for my failure to inspire in my beloved *bechor,* firstborn, a meaningful loyalty to Judaism, for the pain I inadvertently inflicted on my own parents, and because my son has hurt a wonderful young woman who has been unwavering in her love for him. I am weeping because he has announced the end of the dream of closure and healing that I have cherished, however foolishly. Most shattering of all, I am crying because I had hoped to be a mother to a beautiful young Jewish girl (a dancer and an aerialist!), and now for reasons quite extraneous to her or to me, for reasons that have to do with a third party who in this case happens to be my son and not my father, there is once again an irredeemable rupture.

I want to stop this crying and assume some kind of mature equilibrium in front of my son, who is having a hard enough time in his own right. There is even a part of me that wants to comfort and catch my child before he falls. But mostly I am a hurt and fragile human being with all her defenses dissolving around the dining room table. I seek privacy in my room, behind a closed door, hoping to get a handle on my emotions. I know my son will never forgive me for this lavish display of Jewish mother guilt-tripping — and I know that in his place I would probably feel the same — yet there is nothing within my entire repertory of responses that in this moment is going to make me stop bawling.

Finally, I emerge. To cheer me up, or at least to staunch the hemorrhaging, Raphael prattles on a bit about what a great career opportunity this is. His siren, or rather his new lady friend, has already lived and worked out there; all he needs to do is establish residency (with her?) and join the musicians' union, and then he will be able to audition for all sorts of razzle-dazzle roles in Vegas shows. I am hearing all this as if from a great distance. Inside my head there pounds a single *basso ostinato* — no curly-haired, dark-eyed Jewish grandchildren for me, no toddlers running on pattering little feet down the BJ aisle for a sip of sweet grape juice while the beaming rabbi smiles lovingly and holds the Friday night *kiddush* cup high.

This is not going well at all. I can't get a grip on my escalating feelings. From my son's point of view, I am not coming through for him. That is to say, I am evincing no enthusiasm whatsoever for what seems is the end result of a long, tortuous period of deliberation on his part. He needs "some parental blessing." (OMG, did he really use those words?) But rather than extending the coveted good wishes for flourishing along life's path, here I am, visibly melting into a massive puddle. I have been denied the parental blessing, and now I am denying my own child in turn.

It gets worse. He tells me that this glorious new chapter requires only that I find a way to make storage space for all the personal effects he will be leaving behind. He has been doing a lot of sorting through — thoughts, feelings, and of course, material possessions, too. There are things he will need now, and other things that could use a good home in the interim.

In that split second, my meltdown turns into a five-alarm blaze. The rage button has been pushed.

Mom *(to son and the cruel fates, enraged)*: Yes, sure, just go off, destroy everything that matters to me and leave me here with all your stupid stuff.

(Son freezes in a stupefied stare.)

Mom *(beyond the boiling point)*: Do NOT assume that I feel some kind of maternal obligation to make space for all your junk. Why should I have to do that for you?

(Son freezes, afraid he will strike.)

Mom: If you are grown up enough to go off, break hearts, shred illusions, defile dreams, then you are grown up enough to store your own crap.

It gets so bad that neither one of us can see through our hot stinging tears. Neither one of us can control our trembling. Doors are slamming, and I fear some neighbor may decide to call the police, the way they do when the woman across the hall goes off the deep end. I am yelling at him through the slammed door.

"Is there anything of us or my legacy that you cherish?"

After a few moments of silence, he opens the door. I am still standing there, not crossing the threshold. He looks at me steadily and replies: "Your legacy, Mom? What legacy? Your legacy is rage. Why would anyone want to take that along?"

And with that, the door slams again. I am on the outside, in a world gone black. I am wondering how you can make the earth open up and swallow you live, even if you are creating your high drama up on the eighth-floor, while down below, there is nothing but unyielding granite.

Raphael breaks up with Jodi, and though I reach out, she does not return my calls. I am as one who has lost a child, but there is no ritual with which to process this pain. Raphie goes off to Vegas at the siren call of someone else, and naturally, we end up storing a lot of his stuff. I do not attempt to communicate much. This is going to be a long cool-down period, and I am not sure how and when it will end. E.T. takes on the role of intermediary. I don't look for news on Raphie's Facebook page, although I know he gets callbacks at lots of auditions. Soon enough he is even up for the role of lead percussionist in a Vegas production of *The Lion King*.

Then one day he gets the call: He has landed the coveted role. I am over-the-moon proud of his talent and determination. I call to congratulate him because I am thrilled about his achievement. I am also hyper-aware of not reenacting my father's behavior upon receiving important news of my own young life many years ago.

Still, inside there is a hollow. I am muddling through, focusing on what it is I now have to do to move my own life along its path. I go forth worshipping a non-manifest moon. *Rosh Chodesh*, the night of the invisible moon, is, after all, a woman's holiday. Women are expected to have a higher tolerance for the unknown, for the spiritual voids. I know that something will eventually appear and I will see myself reflected in its light, but for now only its outline is vaguely visible.

I can't shake the assumption that returning to Judaism implies accepting the role of human conduit from one generation to another. It can also imply inheriting and passing along a toxic cocktail of unresolved guilt and fear, grief and resultant rage. In her class, Rabbi Uhrbach remarks on the linguistic connections between Abram's imperative to leave his own father and the later imperative to sacrifice his son. She suggests that a spiritual journey might require radical aloneness and an unavoidable severing of ties. A precondition of spiritual evolution is a dedication to the process for our own sakes as individuals. It cannot simply be a propitiation of our ancestors or an assurance for generations to come.

I need to ponder this teaching of hers. Surely it is inadvisable for me to live my Judaism (or my life, for that matter) as the daughter of my parents and the mother of my sons, even if these are the dramas that emotionally inform it the most. A major arc of my life was inspired by my refusal of an inherited obligation to live a certain way, a repudiation of the transpersonal mandate to pass things down. So much of who I am has been forged in self-exile. Now that I am once again reconnected with community, can I still claim my spiritual journey as my own? Does it have a *raison d'être*, regardless of its influence, or lack of same, on my own kids?

I keep attending services at BJ and pursuing my studies of Bible and Talmud. I begin writing for in-house BJ publications while serving on several committees. Outwardly, my life is changing, my commitment is gaining traction, expanding in many ways. Inwardly, I am once again tattered by a sense of rupture; there is so very much to repair.

Vetaheir libainu . . . Purify. Heart. Yours. Theirs. Hers. Mine. His. Mine. His. Mine. His. Mine.

Who can say what it would mean to live now in the full moon of my own heart's truth?

Sitting in an ample, padded lounge chair, I lean back, look up and down a few times, slow my breathing, allow my eyes to soften and close, and invite my focus to turn inwards. Everyone has their own somatic triggers to invite trance; for me, letting the muscles behind closed eyes unwind into a warm swirl, freeing my tongue from my palate, and deepening the breath relax me into the journey. I focus on the sounds in the environment and how my heartbeat is connected to breath. The idea is to slow the mind and draw its attention within, to withdraw into the realm of the deeper regions of self.

The hypnotic modality I embark upon this time is once again a quest for healing and wholeness. In the past, I have experienced journeys in the realm of the unconscious where Older Self comes to dispel some of the alien thought-viruses of the past. This day's journey is a variation on that theme. I am to think of a particularly stubborn behavior pattern to which I am captive. During this journey, the goal is not to manage or control the unwanted pattern, but rather to transform it.

I am working with a deeply imprinted, ruggedly recidivist, hard-wired undesired behavior: my acting out in rage. The first reframe I need is the new understanding that the part of me that operates this behavior firmly believes it is rendering me a vital service. Its worldview might be limited — surely it is stuck in time — but rage's efforts on my behalf come from a positive intention. The path to transformation is through a kind of mediation: I will come to understand what this raging part of me wants and needs. I will honor its objective. Then I will find a way that this same worthy objective can be attained, but by far less costly means.

In this journey, I will conjure a Spirit of Inner Wisdom who will conduct a scripted dialogue with my inner rage. Wisdom will acknowledge the rage response as a commitment to some form of self-protection, and Wisdom will persuade rage that its well-intentioned vigilantism is no longer necessary. That comes about when Wisdom offers access to a core state, or a profound state of well-being. The hypothesis is that once the deep source of well-being is accessed and integrated, there will no longer be a reason for the unwanted behavior, and it will, of its own accord, fade away. I am eager to see for myself how this comes about.

Since all actors in this hypnotic journey get a name, I dub my undesired behavior Inner Rage Energy, addressing her as IRE for short. After a moment's hesitation, I call my Spirit of Inner Wisdom, Chochma. I remember that Chochma holds herself above the fray;

she is unflappable and, unlike Yahweh, she is not implicated in our psychic dramas. *Davke, justement,* that's just it: In this journey, that which is most remote and unchanging will interact with that which is most endemic and reactive. The two will have a little talk, and we will see what emerges from the dialogue.

I need to sink more deeply into the chair, to feel myself unwinding a little more behind the eyes, to feel some warmth surging between my shoulder blades. As my attention turns fully inward, my muscles relax, and I can call upon my inner Chochma to appear in whatever form she chooses.

Soon enough I see a swirling mass approaching from the distance, like the Good Witch who appears in just that way in *The Wizard of Oz.* Chochma is a white swirling mass of energy, with a fragrance of cinnamon and the best myrrh. She is a calm, still voice calling out from the whirlwind.

Now Chochma is hovering over the edge of the deep waters, peering and calling into its depths. She knows that IRE is hiding down there, lurking in her refuge, seeking safety like a small, multi-tentacled sea creature in the crevice of the coral. Chochma is breathing slowly, confidently, audibly, exhaling her sweet fragrance, and as she does, her scented breath sends out a soft ripple across the face of the waters. With every breath she is calling for IRE, cajoling her to come out for a chat.

There is a sharp little splash and a black streak. This is IRE, curious to be sure, but far from convinced that she should show herself on the surface. Chochma is soothing and reassuring, letting IRE know that her good intentions are acknowledged, reiterating that it is known above and below that IRE is working steadily in the name of a good cause. There are just a few details we would like to know a bit more about.

Chochma: Say, IRE, what makes you tick away like a time bomb?
IRE *(after a long silence)*: I have something very important to do.
Chochma: And that is?
IRE: I offer protection from annihilation, a threat that is real and

present at all times.

Chochma: Say more?

IRE: I have to make sure we will not be annihilated by those who doubt our worth, or by those who would discredit us or deny who we really are, or by those who would censure us in any way.

(And I know she perceives that there are many such foes, beginning with the inner circle of my parents, my husband, and my kids. Sometimes the circle expands to include the Jewish community at large.)

Chochma: And you deserve thanks for all the energy you've been putting into this outcome for so many years.

IRE: No annihilation for us, not as long as I am around and on the alert.

(I nod my head and mouth a thank-you even if what I really want to do is point out to Ms. IRE here that her rages have done more to annihilate my self-esteem and threaten my relationships than anything else in my personal repertory of responses. But Chochma urges me to be still and to let the process unfold. This is not the moment to try to talk IRE out of her flawed vigilantism. On the contrary, IRE is needy of my gratitude.)

Chochma: IRE, we honor you. Protection from annihilation is surely a worthy thing. But then tell me, IRE, what is it that protection from annihilation will bring that is even better than protection?

IRE (after a few moments' pause): I want to shut down our detractors.

Chochma: I see. And what does that bring that's even better than shutting down our detractors?

IRE: Revenge . . .

(I think I hear Chochma take in a sharp breath of surprise. But she quickly returns to equanimity and her structured line of inquiry.)

Chochma: And what does revenge bring you that's even better than revenge?

IRE: Reparation for wrongdoing, for all the wrongs committed against us in the past.

Chochma: And what would this reparation bring with it that is even better than reparation?

(Chochma keeps going with this line of questioning, and here are the answers she gets in rapid succession.)

IRE: Reparation brings me justice.

Chochma: And what does justice bring you that's even better than justice?

IRE: What's even better than justice is . . .

. . . for us to exist

. . . for us to feel worthy

. . . for us to be acknowledged

. . . for us to be validated, and okay, why not, honored, too . . .

(Chochma knows that she has to keep delving deeper, to keep following IRE's desires down the outcome chain until she arrives at something abiding, something unconditional and endless, something very much like Chochma herself, something we call a core state.)

Chochma: But tell me, what would validation and honor bring you that's even better than validation and honor?

(It is quiet down here, with only the staccato sound of IRE's little splashes and Chochma's consistent, trusting breath and the whooshing of the waters. After a long pause …)

IRE: We would be Eternal.

(Finally, we are just about hitting the ocean floor, but Chochma wants to see if we can drop down a few more meters.)

Chochma: And what would being Eternal bring that is even better than being Eternal?

IRE: It would bring oneness with God.

Chochma exhales with great satisfaction. Together we have arrived at a core state. We know we are there when we come to a state of well-being that cannot be accomplished or achieved. Rather it is something you simply and utterly are, unconditionally. Core states are expressed in language such as peace, connection, okayness, Divine love, oneness, eternal life force.

Now we are ready for the most important part of the transformation process, the part that makes all the difference. We are asked to accept the idea that we already have this desired core state, that the truth of the matter is that we have always had it, that it is our inalienable Divine blessing from the moment of our birth. Certain causes and conditions have temporarily severed us from this knowledge and given rise to all sorts of acting out. To reclaim this core state, we just have to step into it, to let it reclaim us from its eternal unchanging abode.

So now, still in deep trance, I ask the three parts of myself to fuse into one. I am my own version of Chochma, I am IRE, and I am my mediating self. This reunited self now needs to imagine that the core state, expressed by IRE as a oneness with God, is mine as long as I am ready to receive it. This is the core state that I need to wear lightly and knowingly, like a sacred mantle of assuredness that drapes across my shoulders and envelopes my being. I pause to visualize the core state permeating every cell of my being, embedding itself as a new feature of my emotional coding.

Now I can begin decompressing, slowly ascending, stopping along the way to imagine myself in all the situations where IRE was formerly triggered. I see myself in the crowded BJ balcony the Friday night that man glowered at me and assumed I needed him to straighten me out about the *Shmoneh Esrei* prayer. I remember a conversation after *shabbat* morning services, when a BJ congregant asked me what I thought of a speech given earlier in the day. When I confessed to having arrived too late to hear it, she asked me why I bothered coming at all. I wanted to throttle her. I see myself about to say something of consequence to Roly, being interrupted by another woman who rushes up with a diversionary message. I see myself being criticized by E.T. for having forgotten one item on a grocery list when I remembered everything else. Now the organizer is brushing me off after my visibility presentation at the women's group. Finally, I see myself facing my firstborn, Raphael, and having to hear that he is pushing the destroy button on all of my misplaced dreams.

I see myself in all sorts of situations where heretofore my IRE could be triggered. I re-imagine the IRE-provoking scenes in all their familiar sights, sounds, textures, and smells. But this time I am there cloaked in my new mantle of core transformation. I am there, imbued with a core state. I am there, knowing I am existentially blessed. What will the scene be like now that I have this new resource? How do I respond to whatever happens *if I now know that I am eternally one with God?*

I hear Raphael accusing me of selfishness when he is drumming and I am trying to write. I feel my ever so sorrowful mother telling me that my being-hood is shortening my father's life. I conjure my father thundering his undying curse. I imagine God himself — poor emotionally desperate, unheeded young Yahweh — fuming through his overheated nose, roaring that he will end it all, the whole world as we know it, if people like me don't change their willful ways. I float my way up through it all, aquatic way station by station, this time with the knowing that, in spite of all these limited understandings, the truth is that I, just as I am, in my very being, I do have oneness with God.

And lo and behold, miracle of miracles, IRE, my lifelong companion, no longer feels she needs to attack. With this new spiritual expansion, having let in something more abiding than myself, having allowed myself to be infused with this new knowing, IRE's response is no longer required to keep me intact. Chochma has followed IRE's needs all the way down to their ground-level essence. She has found a way to fulfill IRE's needs, and thanks to this new expanded consciousness, the old route to fulfillment falls into disuse.

I resurface into the room where a group of us are being trained in this hypnotherapeutic technique called Core Transformation, as formulated by Connirae Andreas. As I open my eyes, slowly stretching and anchoring myself in the present place and time, I find myself laughing a little. I'm wondering how the history of Judaism and of the whole world would have been different if someone were to have done this process with a young Yahweh. What if Chochma or Wisdom had stuck by His side and guided Him through this journey?

What if Chochma had whispered to Yahweh that it was not necessary — in fact, it was counterproductive — to breathe fire and drown the world and rant and rage and wreak havoc in order to convince others that he was the One God. What if God the Angry Usurper,

God the Outraged Father, God the Cheated Partner, God the Jilted Lover, God the Defied Lawgiver had been urged by Chochma to get in contact with God the Endless Eternal? God as Angry Agent needed to touch base with God as Divine Truth; in other words, Yahweh needed to inhabit His own core state. If Yahweh could have entered His own core state with certainty, would He not have been less fearful, less fomenting in grief, disappointment, and rage?

There is an *aggada* that says that when the High Priest Ishmael ben Elisha entered the Holy of Holies armed with incense at the most sacred moment of the year, he prayed that God's compassion be evoked to overcome His anger. Unconditional compassion is a core state. Ishmael's blessing is that God will be open to an influx of the core state of Divine compassion. Once this knowing infuses Godly essence, Yahweh's anger can be overcome at last. I once had trouble understanding Avivah Zornberg when she wrote, "To be a source of blessing to God comes to mean to help God achieve his compassionate self." I can now read that teaching with fresh understanding.

It's the second day of Core Transformation hypnosis training, and I am planning to cut out early. It's not that I've reached my saturation point for this kind of deep work. It's just that there is a once-in-a-life-time ceremony scheduled uptown at BJ at 5:00 this Sunday afternoon in May. In celebration of its 180th anniversary, the congregation has commissioned a new Torah scroll. An approved scribe painstakingly handwrites all Torah scrolls in their entirety. It is a long, meticulous labor of love that admits of no errors and takes many months, if not years, to complete. Each of us has been invited to contribute by actually filling in an outlined Hebrew letter or two. Somehow I was out of town when my turn came, so E.T. filled in for me (literally). As it happened, the chosen scribe was a French-speaking Moroccan Jew with whom E.T. unexpectedly bonded, and to my surprise, my Hebraically unlettered husband described the experience as the most profound of his spiritual life.

At the end of the day, the whole congregation is to gather for a special ceremony to escort the completed Torah to the ark with joyous prayers and the special BJ brand of fervent song and dance. In order to make the ceremony on time, I need to leave the downtown hypnosis course about an hour early, a trade-off I am sure will work well all around.

On day one of the training, I very much liked the way Chochma worked with IRE, how Chochma knew to keep delving deeper down the chain of compelling needs until she hit a core state. Chochma can recognize a core state because she herself is one. She knows it's a state of being rather than of having or doing. It is not a state that is dependent on others (so-and-so will love me), nor is it reflexive (I will finally love myself.) It's not even an emotion such as feeling confident, hopeful, or empowered. It is, rather, a pure, unchanging state of being often described by such words as completion, compassion, eternity, oneness, spiritual connection, inner peace. A core state is, to my sensibility, a secular way of articulating that which the mystically inclined call the fullest experience of God.

Now, on the second day of the training, we embark on what Ericksonians call the Parental Timeline Reimprinting. Berta, a warm-hearted woman in her early sixties and a practicing, Israel-trained psychotherapist, volunteers to model the next part of the process. She settles into the big director's chair in front of the classroom and listens as our teacher describes part two of Core Transformation. Suddenly, she grows pale and asks to be excused, explaining that she hadn't realized what this part involves. Considering her personal history, she begs to be disqualified.

This next phase asks that we go back in time and imagine both giving and receiving the fullness of core states — all that unconditional okayness that is ours for the asking — to and from both our parents and grandparents. We need to re-imprint our upbringing by imagining that our parents and grandparents were steeped in the knowledge we now have; we imagine that we have given it to them and that they in turn have re-gifted it to us.

Berta is hastily getting up from her chair, explaining there is no way she can go through it: All four of her Eastern European Jewish grandparents died in Nazi extermination camps. Her parents managed to survive the traumatic events and illegally immigrate to Israel. The incongruity — genocide versus abiding okayness — the screaming gap, the hideous divide is far too radical — impossible, really — to bridge.

The course facilitator acknowledges Berta's reservations and kindly encourages her to do the exercise, not in spite of what she's revealed but because of it. Do I imagine it or does Berta seek my eyes for support? I attach my gaze to hers and mouth the word *davke,* knowing she will understand. I hold her gaze and silently nod in confirmation. She not only can do this — she must.

Berta agrees to go into trance and experience the re-imprinting, the giving and receiving of core states to and from both her embittered orphaned parents and her brutally murdered grandparents. As a group of silent co-travelers, we will offer our own forebears Core Transformation, and with that, create for ourselves a whole new personal history. Is it possible that our boldly creative offering may be received?

I close my eyes and listen to the facilitator guiding Berta through all the necessary steps. I allow myself to time-travel, too, in my own version of the same journey, undertaken on a parallel, if never identical, road.

When the journey is over, we all emerge slowly. It takes a while for me to remember where I am and what day it is. I have been to some place so profound that it is, for the moment, disorienting, like emerging from a kabbalist's waking vision or awakening midafternoon from a brief sleep drenched in the transcendent images of the unconscious. I cannot now simply take my leave of this place and these people, even if not doing so means I will miss a part of the BJ ceremony. What we have experienced, Berta and I and the others, needs to be integrated in reverential silence. We must remain quietly present in its wake. If I did not until now know how transformation manifests in the body — the tingling skin, released muscles, cascading chills and hot inner core, the post-orgiastic afterglow — now I know it for sure.

The Shoah, the most radical expression of our rupture with the unfeeling Divine, is present here, sharing the same small space with the Divine now experienced as transformational healer. In kabbalistic terms, the harrowing experience of *tsimtsum*, God's self-contraction and utter withdrawal, is being infused with the healing power of *hitpashtut*, an overflowing of Divine energy. Core Transformation comes about when the abiding and unconditional core state that the religious call God is allowed to heal humanity's most profound pain. We are inviting the terror of ultimate abandonment to meet this emanation of Divine love. Berta offered this healing energy to her brutalized parents and grandparents. In our hypnotic journey — call it wild imagination, call it fervent prayer, call it mystical vision — there was an experience of acceptance. Thus a new template of possibility was impressed upon our very souls. Out of the vertigo of radical contradictions, from the nexus of untenable opposites, in the gap between annihilation and redemption, I feel the distinctive stirring of a new yearning.

I have received something life-changing from the Source, and now I would like to reciprocate. That is to say, I want to offer back to the Source the same gift it has just given me. *And you will love* . . . in a loving relationship it is not enough to cherish an intense, private experience. The irresistible impulse is to communicate and to share. I have been recharged, and I would like the transcendent to be recharged by me, in turn. I am asking God, too, to return from exile and to share in my homecoming. How can I offer the privilege and grace of transformational healing to *no-am zivuch*, to the Endless Radiance that is its very Source?

We know that God is sometimes separated from His/Her own heart. But in moments of Divine inwardness, there can be movement from frustration to acceptance, from agitation to peace, from wrath to compassion. Sometimes, as in the Ishmael High Priest story, it is fragrance that is the agent of the shift in God's inner life. However it comes about, *ah na el na,* please God, keep unfolding. If my evolution is within the realm of possibility, let its gifts hasten the healing of the fractured Divine. As Zornberg has said, perhaps I can truly become a blessing at last, by guiding, in my own small way, God to his compassionate self.

And you will love . . . I want God to believe that our uneasy romance could, in fact, end well. I pray God to shift from despair to knowing, I invite the Divine to share in my vision of a hopeful outcome. I imagine God overcoming his untamed fear and its resulting wrath when he indwells in the unconditional consciousness of Chochma, the mind-body anti-*gezera* wisdom of Miriam and the other feminine prophets whose voices have been stilled. Together with these women, I echo the Psalm, "Let him take hold of my strength that he may make peace with me."

Slowly I take my leave of the downtown classroom. I am moving unhurriedly, yet I am in a big rush. It is late on a Sunday afternoon in May; I conclude that a taxi would be more reliable than the irregular weekend subway. But I am mistaken. As is true every Sunday in spring, the city streets are hopelessly snarled with traffic detoured from street fairs, parades, and all the resulting closed thoroughfares. I spend fully half an hour in a stalled cab trying to get crosstown at 14th Street. Every time we turn north, we advance a few streets and then find the same impasse as soon as we try to make our way west. Another uptown thoroughfare flows freely for a few blocks and is suddenly barricaded. Four lanes of traffic take forever to merge into one. I may have experienced transformation, but the path between the welcoming of the Torah and me is hideously clogged.

What cruel irony has decreed that after the gifts of this day, I be barred from joining the others in joyous celebration of a brand new co-created Torah? Is there still some lingering force that is keeping me from the liberation I seek? I had not expected to be thwarted on this Transformational Day. I had expected all barriers to fall and my path to be clear.

Feeling fatigued, loath to focus on a snarled city, I lean back and close my eyes. I wonder if I will be able to create an essential-oil blend that anchors and recalls this new core state. I will delve into it, I will experiment with frankincense, cinnamon, sandalwood, and myrrh.

Using these sacred oils, I want to create something I'll call CoreEssence and share its healing fragrance with others.

Through the now-porous barrier separating layers of mind, a familiar image arises. My father, my mother, my brother, my maternal grandparents, all of whom I knew and loved, join hands in a circle dance. The circle has expanded to include me, E.T., Raphael, and Jonathan. We levitate off the ground, no longer bound by the laws of gravity, and we go round and round. This dance is not linear, it does not progress, it does not follow a serpentine path or trace its route to anywhere. It just goes round and round, and we are all equidistant from the center. I realize that this is Miriam's dance, taught to me long ago by the living Shulamite. This is a woman's sacred rite, a mystical enactment known as the Celestial Round.

Zornberg describes the Celestial Round as a "supreme condition of spiritual consciousness." It is in this dance that Miriam draws down the transcendent light. I think back to the song "*Yedid Nefesh*," You Who Love My Soul, and to Moses' prayer for his sister: *Ah na el na,* please God, *refah na la,* do heal her. And how might she be healed? The song responds: By the drawing down of the transcendent light. Zornberg tells us it is "the dance that generates the light," and in this dance "the women produce an energy in the light of which all participate equally in the presence of God." Each of the dancers is a conduit for the radiant light from the other realm. Each of the dancers is a vessel for the core state, the very one we have been journeying to.

This drawing down of supreme light is something deeply personal; Zornberg calls it "an intimate awareness writ large." We open to the unconditional core state, and in that moment, "a claim is made on eternity." The soul's deepest longing is satisfied, even or especially as "the people still tread the precarious floor of the sea."

More than one hour later, we are once again stalled as we inch toward the intersection of 72nd Street and Broadway. I pay the exorbitant taxi fare and get out and run. I am some fifteen blocks away from BJ, but now it's best to rely on my two legs to carry me where I need to go. I must be careful not to twist my ankle, alarmingly wobbly in my flimsy heeled mules. I will be careful not to be toppled by a hidden crack in the sidewalk. The streets are crowded with pedestrian as well as vehicular traffic, and the warm city air is thick with humidity. My blouse sticks to my chest, my pores feel filthy and clogged. I still have a good ten uptown blocks and one westward block to run. I can count on my stamina, but my breathing is labored and I am soaking in sweat.

Finally, panting and parched, I slip into the packed sanctuary, forced by the crowds to stand at the back. I see the Torah has already been returned to the ark. I have missed the ceremony, the accompanying procession, all the music and the dance. I can see Roly way up front, and hear Joseph's voice holding the final notes longer than any of the others. I catch a glimpse of E.T. His face is glowing.

I have missed all, except for one song: I join in as we sing *Hashiveinu venashuva,* return us and we shall be returned. *Chadesh yameinu kekedem,* renew us as in days of old. I am not too late for this song; even if my portion is reduced, it will be sufficient for me at this time. It will be perfect; it will be mine. I raise my voice in communion with a thousand others, and I know with a core certainty this is the song meant for me.

How Has It Come to This?

Afterword

How can I articulate, much less defend, an attachment to a religious heritage that has for decades lived side by side with a strong aversion? How to explain devotion to a religious tradition that has historically excluded me as a woman from its principal activities of study and prayer?

Recently, I discovered that Jewish wisdom has something to say about the attraction/avoidance dynamic, or the codependence of opposites.

Abraham Isaac Kook, one of the 20th century's most influential rabbis, spoke of a synergy that develops when navigating between opposite poles. One point of view would not retain its vitality were it not for the opposing pull of its contrary. Rav Kook encouraged us to pray for the survival of those whose views oppose ours, for in that way we not only charge up our own argument but also fuel the very debate that Judaism relies upon to bring us closer to truth. His wisdom regarding interpersonal disputes guides me in managing the polarities warring within.

I was raised within an elaborate Jewish cocoon of myth-making. Myth is not a falsification of truth. Rather, it is a construct of metaphoric meaning by which to read the human experience. There is a great deal we need to read and relate to, beginning with our birth into a certain family with all its lore. Soon enough we face the imperative to organize time, the need for grounding in some ethical system, then the quest for a worthy occupation, while concerns about ego and mortality, sexuality, and fear of annihilation haunt us all our days. Love and loss, speculations as to our place in the cosmos, and encounters, however ambivalent, with ultimate concerns are also integral to the human condition.

If deprived of opportunities to wrestle with all that Jewish tradition has to contribute to these spheres, I am diminished; I am cut off from my ancestors and alienated from a deep part of myself.

My big discovery is that non-allegiance to a fixed version of religious reality is no barrier to entry. I am a modern day re-mythologizer who speaks from within a rich tradition that remains in some ways viable and in many other ways in need of reconsideration.

If ever I am called upon — as I hope never to be — to testify, I will confess to not taking these Jewish myths as literal truths. A chosen people, a brokered covenant, emancipation from Egypt, revelation at Sinai, manna from Heaven, a just God who intervenes in history — all of this functions for me as grist for the meaning-making mill that keeps churning within. The myths of the Jewish tradition deserve careful attention. For me, they are inspiring to the degree that they remain dynamic, provocative, and receptive to contemporary midrashic interpretation. The Jewish take on life's rhythms and purpose is attractive to me for the edgy discussion it never fails to spark.

Recently, I visited Israel with a BJ group under the leadership of Rabbi Roly. The trip focused on study, and its theme was prayer. Early in the week, Roly introduces us to Rabbi Tamar Elad Applebaum, a petite, vivacious woman who hails from a venerable Moroccan family. Tamar had to break away from her family's sexist Orthodoxy in order to claim her place as a spiritual leader, both in their patriarchal clan and in the broader community. On the day that one of her children was born, she told her ancient grandfather that she had been ordained as a rabbi (some six years after the fact). He was a man who assumed women would forever remain servile, happy to prepare their lavish feasts while men studied and prayed.

Still, the elder listened to what Tamar had to say. There was a silence. Then he replied. "I do not know what a woman rabbi is. I have never heard of such a thing. But I know you are someone of spiritual depth, someone who loves prayer and study and the Jewish people. I assume all will be well."

One of the most worn-out Jewish myths is that God is closer to men than he is to women. Women hover in the background when the covenant is cut by a man into the genitals of an eight-day-old male. How could a woman, deprived of inclusion and education, assume a religious leadership role? Tamar gave her grandfather an opportunity to reconsider that myth along with the social order it dictates, and to everyone's surprise, he took it.

Rabbi Tamar asks us with a twinkle in her eye if we can identify the very first prayer. It was God's, says she, in the opening chapter of Genesis: "Let there be light." This gives us permission "to constantly create something beyond what is seen, beyond what is known." Orthodoxy is the known paradigm, particularly on the Israeli religious scene. But Tamar, now a post-denominational rabbi, is searching for a revitalized form of Judaism that brings not more words or abstract ideas or rules, but "a new connection with life."

We ask ourselves daily, what does it really mean to choose life? To do good? To promote blessing? What is the place of our passions in this schema? What about our curiosity about a world beyond the Jewish ken? What responsibility do we have to the future of the planet and to people who are not of our tribe?

I ask myself if there is anything inherently Jewish about the answers we bring to these crucial questions. We know that in the past, the world has experienced some vital paradigm shifts thanks to the contributions of our people, however tiny our numbers. What would be today's equivalent of instituting the Sabbath as a weekly day of rest or declaring Thou Shall Not Kill? What is our part in bringing a new moral perspective to the world table? What kind of example do we set with some of our current political stances in the Middle East? Do we have the solidarity, the staying power, and commitment to make an impact? What price, if any, are we willing to pay? The reply entails a constant process of self-refinement, demanding increasingly profound levels of honesty about what really matters. Engagement with the BJ community insures that we keep up this conversation.

Rabbi Tamar emphasized the importance of feeling free to explore. To do that I need to feel safe, even as I enter a place where I once felt fundamentally threatened. The central organizing pole of my existence, the ladder between Heaven and Earth that Tillich calls "the ultimate concern," is situated in *ha'makom ha'zeh*, in this place and in this tradition into which it was my destiny to be born.

Nobody ever said that this ladder wasn't going to be shaky.

Not long ago, I pitched a book about Talmudic aggada *to the editor* of a prominent publishing house. I entertained her with a lively spiel about *aggada's* richness of insight, its unabashed quirkiness and delight in paradox, its knowledge of human nature alongside its post-modern avoidance of conclusions.

Specifically, I proposed a book about the aggadic stories of women that pop up throughout the rabbinic literature. Some women, like Bruriah or Homa, are named, while the majority are known only as wife of a certain man, or mother, daughter, sister of another. Each of these women — however nameless, muted, and veiled — comes to disrupt the male-dominated equilibrium. The rabbinic response to them varies, as do the women's skills in provoking new insight.

The publisher was skeptical that such a book could find a market. She argued that progressive women don't care about the Talmud, and Orthodox women don't want to hear my take on it. While I saw it differently, I was in no position to prove her wrong.

Before ending our meeting, I brought up the editor's well-known affinity for the Lower East Side. I mentioned that my own family, like hers, has its roots there. When I went on to identify my paternal grandfather, Rabbi Yosef Dov Reimer, she caught her breath sharply, possibly in disbelief, surely in surprise. Her own grandparents were friends and admirers of his, and she was brought up to revere my grandfather, much as I was. (It was a highly charged moment, but didn't persuade her to sign me on.)

When I tell the tale to Rabbi Jan Uhrbach at BJ the next day, she agrees that in his human incarnation, this grandfather might not have approved of my version of Judaism or of me. But then Jan, a former star corporate lawyer, shares her personal belief about the experience of souls during their sojourn in the World to Come: They keep on evolving. It is, says Jan, my grandfather in a spiritually expanded version of himself who visited me in the editor's office that day. She encourages me to keep becoming who I am meant to be so that he, too, can keep evolving.

I never did convince the editor to let me write about women in the *aggada*. I will, however, continue studying these cryptic, undervalued tales, especially now when conflict over gender roles is provoking a furor in the Jewish community. The Orthodox and the progressives have very different points of view about what's at stake. All agree: a great deal. My idea is to defuse and decode the present-day conflict via a study of these literary texts. The Talmud's take on gender issues and the social fabric of the community is a perfect springboard for interdenominational discussion.

These days, Rabbi David Silber and I converse comfortably, enjoying many shared references from our past. He is the founder of Drisha, an institution founded some thirty years ago to serve the educational needs of Orthodox women, and now, the broader community. I look forward to the soon-to-be-launched Drisha course on *aggada* and some day to have Roly team-teach there in an atmosphere of open inquiry.

Now and then, as these efforts take shape, I think it possible that my Talmudic grandfather and I are getting to experience one another in a whole new way.

There is an aggada *in the Talmud about a rabbi who has a compulsive* attraction to prostitutes. One day, he hears of a woman who is reputed to be the most beautiful of all. He fills a bag with gold coins and crosses seven rivers to find her. When finally they lie together, she farts. Says she to him, "You are no more likely to find absolution than is this gas likely to return to my body."

For him, it is an ah-ha! moment. He begs the mountains, the heavens, the sun, the moon, and the stars to intercede for him, but they all refuse in turn. Finally, realizing that atonement is up to him alone, he sits down with his head between his knees, and from the depths of his being, cries himself to a remorseful death. The Good Lord takes him up to Heaven and declares him worthy of the World to Come. Others who have spent their entire lives doing good deeds cannot always count on such an outcome.

I was taken by surprise last spring when, during her annual U.S. lecture tour, Avivah Zornberg ended one of her talks by citing this baffling story. Months later, she and I are having coffee in Jerusalem. I ask her why she wove in that *aggada,* and she replies that in the context of her remarks (on the petition of Zelophechad's daughters in Numbers 27) she wanted to give an example of a person who wins eternal life in a nanosecond, while others, apparently far more righteous, often struggle for years to no such avail.

Avivah tells me this at a time when I am looking back and projecting forward and trying to assess a whole panoply of life choices. On this, my first trip to Israel in fifteen years, in the days before I go up to Jerusalem, I walked the beaches and boulevards of Tel Aviv, recalling that time, now nearly thirty-five years ago, when I contemplated the direction of my life as a young, single woman eager for a man and motherhood. There were no lack of offers from Israelis, no dearth of introductions and blind dates. But on the way over to my six-month stint with the Bat Dor dance company, I had already encountered E.T. on the Parisian sidewalk en route to the dinner party a few flights up.

At the time, I shared my inkling about the Instant Recognition Alert with a few friends in Israel, but hardly any took me seriously. There is such a thing as a moment of profound knowing. There is even, in my playbook, such a thing as Higher Intelligence, guiding the invisible interconnections of destiny. But whether or not all that follows — the subsequent deeds and events playing out from the decisive moment — magnify a blessing is a lot more complicated to assess. I have never regretted my marriage to E.T. and will forever marvel at our two sons. But like most other mortals, we — he and I — constantly review our choices and keep struggling for an unlikely version of redemption.

Several weeks before I left on the Israel trip, my son Raphael returned from two years of a worldwide tour as a musician with the Cirque de Soleil, following his success in *The Lion King.* We have been in touch only irregularly. Since the breakup with Jodi, he has been through several relationships, all with women not of our tribe. He is currently unattached, eager to redirect his life from performing to composing. Towards that end, he wants to live awhile under the radar, attending school in his newly chosen field while he learns a whole new set of skills.

Not long after his arrival, during the break on Yom Kippur afternoon, when the four of us have been fasting for some twenty hours, Raphael suddenly lambastes me about the toxic rage I have passed on, even though I have not had an eruption in quite a long time. I am shaken to my core, trying to find an explanation for his continued pain and hostility. Perhaps he is suffering a sugar low, perhaps it is combined with jet lag and withdrawal from nicotine and whatever other substances he may have been using while living with circus people on the road. I am at a loss. But his anger, self-destructive and tearful, rages even after we break the fast at several congenial gatherings.

The assault is such that we feel the fabric of our family in tatters, and each of us is desperate and grieving. I go off to Israel some six weeks later with the heaviest of unhealed *mamele* hearts, ambivalent about the chosen theme of prayer. I am suspicious of any easy fix, yet open to a path that will shed light and heal.

A few weeks earlier, also at Yom Kippur time, I heard David Silber speak of bad deeds giving birth to bad angels who then give birth to more of their kind in an unfortunate chain of what might be called karmic events. Someone in the room assumed laughingly that a man of Rabbi Silber's discernment could not possibly believe in such fanciful lore. David countered that he most certainly did. I think of what my mother had to say about the good and bad angels who accompany us home from the synagogue every Sabbath. I think of some of the choices I made when raising my own children, and I pray on the eve of what the French call *Le Grand Pardon* that more good angels can still be generated from the seeds of our belated good deeds.

Roly designed the Jerusalem trip to introduce us to his own chevruta, a group of scholars, educators, and thought leaders who most inspired his months of study during his recent sabbatical. Our mission is to make connections between Jews such as ourselves and Jews in Israel who share a devotion to an open, pluralistic spirituality as a healing alternative to the increasing polarization between religious and secular extremists in both lands.

On the second day of our Jerusalem seminar, Roly introduces us to a teacher named Rabbi Dov Zinger. He is tall, with a long white beard, and is clearly of the paradigmatic Orthodox Male Establishment. I learn that he lives in the Occupied Territories and leads a male-only, fervent *yeshiva* whose expansionist politics would surely clash with our own. But he is part of the group that is dedicated to religious revival in Israel. This *chevruta's* commitment to pluralism means there is room for all, even those who do not think as they do. Last year, I am told, when the BJ group went to Rav Dov's *yeshiva*; the women were requested to dress modestly in skirts. They all did. This year, he has come to us, and we women are dressed as we please.

Rav Dov wants to talk about the shortest and most concentrated verbal formula for prayer to be found in the Bible. It is none other than *El na refah na la,* five highly charged words that find their way into the *"Yedid Nefesh"* song and have their origins in the Book of Numbers. I remark that I find it difficult to ignore the sexist context in which this prayer arises. When God afflicts Miriam with leprosy as punishment for her speaking out against Moses, God's response to Moses' plea for her restored health has to do with fathers spitting in their daughters' faces. Rav Dov thanks me for providing context but cordially ignores my objections.

There is an exercise he invites us to do. We will work with these five words: *El na refah na la.* We are to leave the two words *"na"* as they are. Depending on what it is we are praying for, we can recompose the other three words. *"El,"* which means God, can be retitled in a way that aligns us with the specific aspect of God we are addressing.

I am remembering something another teacher named Uri told us the day before. Hailing from a Hasidic background, Uri shared with us the origin of the *nigun,* the wordless melody that in Hasidic tradition can lift celebrants to the highest rungs of devotion. How, he asked us, does a *nigun* come to be? He replied that every time we are able to see a Divine spark in someone with whom we are locked in difficulty, from that insight a new *nigun* is born.

My prayer is for my percussionist son, for whom music is the path to alignment both with his highest self and with all that is right with the world. In my prayer for Raphael, *El* or God becomes *"Mekor Ha'-nigunim"* or Source of All Melodies. I add *"na nagen na bo,"* which simply means "please play Your music within him."

We are asked to read our prayer aloud to the group, I recite the prayer slowly. The second time, I am asked to invite the group to join me in reciting a chosen portion of the prayer. I ask the others to join in on the words *"na nagen na,"* and they do. I soak in the empowerment of community and say "amen."

Later that day, I take a long walk from the Hartman Institute to the Old City and wind my way through the bustling market to the site of the Temple Mount. I write the prayer down on a piece of paper and, with no self-consciousness, slip it into the Wailing Wall. I walk away from the Wall with backward steps, not in any hurry to turn my back on the highly charged site.

I am aware that it was with a variation of those same words that my crushed and fear-laden father once prayed for me.

On Thursday morning towards the end of our week in Jerusalem, a Kabbalah scholar named Dr. Melila Heiner Eshed comes to teach us about inclusion and exclusion, basing her lesson on the Book of Ruth. I have never forgotten how Roly's invitation for me to speak of my take on the Ruth story at the all-night Shavuot gathering moved me towards center from the self-imposed margin. I now see how my rapprochement mirrored the stranger Ruth's moving in from the pariah fringe.

How come you can see me? That's what Ruth says to Boaz in the field. What's more, she asks him how it is that he fully recognizes and accepts her in all her otherness. Boaz sees Ruth for exactly who she is, and she is grateful for his gaze. Melila says, "To really be seen in your uniqueness, to drop pretense but keep your identity, this is *ge'ula.*" *Ge'ula* is a Hebrew word for "redemption." Redemption requires overcoming the way in which vulnerability induces an undercurrent of shame that shuts you down. It implies getting comfortable with vulnerability in a way that allows you to be open. It asks for a reconsideration of one's own strengths and weaknesses along with those of a complex tradition once left behind.

For some time, I have been a member of a BJ-based study group. We began with Zornberg, moved on to Art Green, and are now reading *Sacred Fragments* by Neil Gilman. Catching up with Gilman's book after time away, I come across his take on the importance of myth and focus especially on what he has to say about a myth once it is broken: "A myth can be broken and still live because there is no alternative to myth making. The issue is never myth or no myth, but which myth. For myth is the only means available to us for comprehending complex and elusive dimensions of our experience."

A myth that is surely broken within the Jewish world is the one that expresses a patriarchal view about the origins, nature, status, privileges, and capacities of women. This is the issue that I understand is keeping even (or especially) Orthodox rabbis up at night. They need to wrestle with the inevitability of change within a hierarchical system that has long remained static. They need to honestly assess the extent to which the separate and unequal status of women is indivisible from the profound truth of Orthodox Judaism, as apart from considerations for its social order. How can change continue to come about without complete destabilization? Even more urgently — how can it not?

For non-halachic, if religious, feminists like me, the questions are a little different: Are women now seeking full rights and unrestricted access to the traditional world as we have inherited it from men? Or do we, in order to fully integrate women's experiences into Jewish life, have to inaugurate a far more radical transformation? I side with the second scenario. I wonder how Judaism will change now that more and more women are actively writing themselves back into the male-formulated story. How close can we come to what Judaism would look like had it been articulated and systematized along the way by anti-*gezera* women in the first place? On the political front, how can we respond to men who, recoiling from the alleged "feminization"of liberal sectors, take retro-flight into Orthodoxy? It makes me grateful and even a little giddy to be rejoining the conversation at such an effervescent and critical time.

Some years back, I wondered if the right remedy for what ailed me might not be detachment from my personal narrative. If I could forget about being labeled Not Such a Good Girl, about the eruption that was the late 1960s and '70s, the wrath of a father, self-exile, and on and on, might I find a quieter space inside, more receptive to some larger truths?

Today I look at the question differently. I assign significance, as I believe others should, to the contours of my personal journey. Each of our paths is traced and enshadowed, chastised and ennobled, misguided and illuminated by our individual character and choices, our temperament and preferences. In fact, all of religious experience is filtered through some human experience or perception. The life story of each one of us is the stuff religious experience is made of.

After all, the Bible does not begin with the laws of Leviticus for good living. It begins instead with a foundational creation myth and then zooms right in on individual characters, all of whom have to live a human life before they can arrive at abiding religious insight. Their stories encourage us to chart our own, using theirs, when appropriate, as models.

In this endeavor, I wander freely in a post-gender zone. I am Miriam, questioning male authority and leading others in dance. I am Jacob, and also his son Joseph, both seeking closure with families they left behind many years before. I see parts of myself in all of these Maybe Not Such Good Girls. I am Ruth, astonished by the blessing of really being seen. I am Bruriah, carving out a place at the study hall table. I am Homa, forever using her feminine wiles. I am Rachel, refusing comfort when praying for the welfare of her sons. I empathize, too, with the

High Priest Elisha, entering the inner sanctum with a humble stick of fragrant incense and praying on behalf of myself, my father, my son, and a broken God, that the capacity for loving-kindness conquer our weakness for rage.

A few of the women from my New York study group want to hear about my Israel experience in greater detail. They ask me in particular how I felt about the Orthodox Rav Dov.

In this group we have already discussed the broken myth of petitionary prayer; that is to say, we no longer believe (if we ever did) that as long as we are good and ask nicely, God will fulfill our needs. But on one early winter *shabbos* afternoon, after we have shared a meal and sung a few songs, I confide in these women my troubles with my son and my composition of the five-word prayer. (Despite our shared skepticism, they all nod with empathy when I tell of slipping the paper into the Wall.)

I go on to the next part of the story. I tell them that I am repeating that private prayer often, though not at any fixed times. At first it opened a wellspring of bitter tears, but I stuck with it, eventually relishing the catharsis. I remark that gradually, whenever I recited those five words, I felt better aligned with some serene part of myself that believed in the rightness of my son's path. It also put me in touch with an internal source that, in spite of hurt and anxiety, could love unconditionally.

It was only a matter of days before I learned of a shift. The e-mails coming from Raphael began to take on an entirely different tone. He was calm and concerned about others, reaching out with affection, and far less agitated. He was settling into his studies and hearing music in a whole new way.

Some Jewish thinkers speak of God as the capacity each of us has to seek and awaken the Divine spark within and evolve into our highest selves. Coming closer to the overbearing God of our history may, in the 21st century, increasingly be about finding ways to awaken the inner evolutionary impulse, which some would say is synonymous with relating to the Divine. That intention has to do with refining our capacity for empathy and trust, and in whatever way has meaning for us, opening to the beloved, however frequently we miss the assignation.

How has it come to this? The zealot's runaway daughter . . . she who broke her parents' heart, she who turned her back, she who defined herself as an agent of rupture and refusal . . .

It is 8:30 on a *shabbat* morning in early December, and a cold wind whips up from the Hudson River at the intersection of 86ᵗʰ Street and West End Avenue. I am just one block from the apartment that for twelve years now has been my uncontested and much-cherished home. I am about to cross over to the corner church of St. Andrews and St. Paul, whose premises BJ still shares, and slip into the smaller chapel where chairs have already been arranged in a circle and Roly is teaching the ingathered to sing a beloved *piyyut*.

How has it come to this? Suzi Maybe Not Such a Good Girl, who always made an appearance just before the service was about to end, is joining this intimate group in the morning hour before *shabbat* prayers even begin.

A *piyyut* is a liturgical poem characterized by mystical longing, part of a prayer literature extant since the days of the Temple. This early morning, "*Yedid Nefesh,*" You Who Love My Soul, is our first *piyyut*. My emotional tremor is still real but much muted. Roly is not teaching us the Ashkenazi melody I always sang with my father; he is, rather, teaching us two melodies, one from Morocco and the other from Iraq. It takes me time to adjust to their warbling plaintiveness, also to let go of a certain longing for the way I once harmonized these same words around the *shabbos* table with my dad. By now I know that allowing for the next phase of spiritual growth is neither about avoiding the past nor clinging to it with exaggerated attachment.

I am growing accustomed to hearing *"Yedid Nefesh"* in unfamiliar arrangements. Music was an integral part of our exploration of prayer while in Jerusalem. One night, we went to a specially commissioned concert performed by post-modern musicians whose theme was "Songs of the Sabbath." There we heard *"Yedid Nefesh"* and a whole range of other *shabbat* songs deconstructed, fragmented, silenced in usual places of gusto, with anticipated flow broken into staccato and incongruous rhythms. One song dissolved into another as if all the Jews the world over were now neighbors, singing around their *shabbos* tables, audible through ceiling and floor and eerily thin walls, all of them harmonizing and counterpointing through a sleepless, sanctified night.

I let go into feeling unmoored in this realm that Zornberg likes to call "the known unknown." It is the realm of the unconscious, of the religious imagination, and of dreams. It is the place that tempts with slippage into worlds apart from the everyday; it is the place that beckoned and frightened me on the evening of *Slichot*. At such vertiginous times, it is good to weave my voice into the steadying chorus of community who are winding their way through the mysterious music of *piyyut* and of life. I return to the song we sang every Friday night around the *shabbat* table.

For then she will be healed and then she will be whole
Hasten, show love,
Surely the time is now.

Acknowledgments

Like most spiritual quests, mine took place in the space between isolation and belonging. Looking back on the decade chronicled in this memoir, I see my return to the fullness of progressive Jewish life as a gift from all the extraordinarily people who helped me along the way.

Personal renewal begins when someone else comes along and holds up a mirror. Gradually, another image of the self comes into wavering focus. Rabbi J. Roland Matalon and Dr. Avivah G. Zornberg were the first to perceive and reflect back hidden facets of my inner self. Ronald Guttman is another seeker who glimpsed my Jewish soul even as we navigated secular seas. Their support and *chesed* are the cornerstones of all that has followed.

There were many other teachers along the way. Rabbi Art Green articulated many of my nascent views. Rabbi David Silber of Drisha let me know that sometimes it really is possible to come home again, albeit in an unpredictable way. Rabbi Jan Uhrbach is a woman who I always count upon to take the philosophical journey one step further.

Sheila Schwartz, in what was to be the last year of her life, told me I must write after many years of inactivity. Lawrence Bush of JEWISH CURRENTS, editor and publisher of this book, supported my evolution from blogger to author every step of the way. Sandee Brawarsky of the *Jewish Week* is a tireless friend and advocate who consistently offered outlets for my work.

The women of the Me'Az group bring a special safety, sweetness and seriousness to our shared study. Their supportive presence as seekers and friends infuses the word "sisterhood" with new meaning. Our *shabbat* afternoon gatherings bring deep serenity and insight. Of that cherished group, I especially want to thank Ilene Richman, my *chevruta* partner, for her willingness to entertain my questions, flights of fancy and doubts.

Joan Roth, who has been photographing Jewish women all over the world for decades, honored me by taking my back-cover portrait, and with her partnership on some timely photo-reportage and exciting joint projects still to come.

Anne Millman has my gratitude for her stalwart and wise help in bringing this book — and all that I have to offer — to the attention of a wider world.

Paul Veres, a former schoolmate of Anne's, a gifted man I have met only through e-mails, designed the book cover in an act of generosity and creativity that makes me feel so blessed.

Deborah Brissman's eagle-eyed proofing prepared this manuscript to meet the larger world scrubbed clean of inconsistencies, and lavished with the kind of detailed care that only she could provide. A single mom with a full-time job, her candle burned late into the night.

Joan Hochman, Rabbi Felicia Sol, Esther Cohen, Amy Stone of *Lilith* magazine, Elana Sztokman, Lilli Platt, Susan Elephante, Susan Kippur, Jeannie Blaustein, Alexis Sasanow, Jordan Reimer, Ziva Reimer Hassenfeld, Mim Warden, Dina Mann, Susan Rollins, Paul Geltner, Jonathan Rosen, Jessica Shapiro, Fern Flamberg, and the Jewish Book Council all helped me in exactly the ways I needed when the time was right.

Joan Westreich's 24/7 wisdom, friendship and therapeutic love have always given me faith in myself, most especially when reserves were low.

My brother Joseph Reimer has always been the lighthouse illuminating a safe return to what were once distant shores.

My two adult children, Raphael and Jonathan, continue to reveal me to myself in challenging, encouraging, and miraculous ways. Like all *mameles* of the world, it is in them that my spirit forever ventures forth.

And most of all, my thanks go to E.T., without whom my life

is impoverished, be it in the Old World or the New. The Universal Mover really had something in mind when S/He arranged to have us bump into one another that day on a Parisian sidewalk. Thank you, E.T., for cutting my grapefruit every morning and sharing every byway of the exhilarating, sacred adventure we call life.

This book is dedicated to my parents, Mildred Ruth Reimer and Philip Meyer Reimer, whose values, passion, and dedication made me who I am.

About the Author

The dissident daughter of an Orthodox Jewish family, Susan Reimer-Torn spent twenty-two years raising a family in France, avoiding communal life and writing for the *International Herald Tribune* on dance, culture, and spiritual undercurrents in a self-consciously secular Europe. Since her return to New York in 2001, she has become a life coach and hypnotherapist while writing about Jewish feminist issues for a variety of publications *(www.susanreimertorn.com)*. In our time of self-questioning and religious renewal, Susan delights in probing conversation, and facilitates workshops about self-realization for women within an evolving Jewish world.